PSYCHIC
EMPOWERMENT
FOR EVERYONE

Lisa Novak

CARL L. WESCHCKE is the Chairman of Llewellyn Worldwide, Ltd., one of the oldest and largest publishers of New Age and occult books in the World. Weschcke (a Magician, Student of Tantric Philosophy and of Western Magic, and former Wiccan High Priest) played a leading role in the rise of Wicca and Neo-Paganism during the 1960s and 1970s, purchasing Llewellyn Publications in 1960.

A life-long student of a broad range of New Age and Occult subjects, Weschcke has studied with the Rosicrucian Order, the Society of the Inner Light, and continues with studies and practical research in Tantra, Taoism, Kabalah, Astrology, Shamanism, Wicca, Magic, Psychology, and Spirituality.

In addition to an academic degree in business administration, he has a certificate in clinical hypnosis, and honorary recognitions in divinity and magical philosophy.

Currently he is devoting most of his activity to studies in quantum theory, Kabbalah, self-hypnosis, and psychology, and to writing.

This volume is the first of several books which Weschcke is collaborating on with Dr. Slate.

Warren H. McLemore

JOE H. SLATE is a licensed psychologist in private practice and Professor Emeritus at Athens State University. As head of the Psychology Department and Director of Institutional Effectiveness, he established the University's parapsychology research laboratory and introduced parapsychology into the curriculum, a first for the state of Alabama. His research has been funded by the U.S. Army, the Parapsychology Foundation of New York, and numerous private sources. He founded the International Parapsychology Research Foundation which has endowed scholarships programs in perpetuity at both Athens State University and the University of Alabama.

Slate holds a Ph.D. from the University of Alabama, with post-doctoral studies from the University of California. He is Honorary Professor at the University of Montevallo where he participated in the university's curriculum development efforts. He is a member of the American Psychological Association and a Platinum Registrant in the National Register of Health Service Providers in Psychology. He is a frequent lecturer and has appeared on numerous radio and TV programs including Sightings and Strange Universe. His research on the human energy system was recently featured on History TV's *Vampire Mysteries*.

TO WRITE TO THE AUTHORS

If you wish to contact the authors or would like more information about this book, please write to the authors in care of Llewellyn Worldwide and we will forward your request. The authors and publisher appreciate hearing from you and learning of your enjoyment of this book and how it has helped you. Llewellyn Worldwide cannot guarantee that every letter written to the authors can be answered, but all will be forwarded. Please write to:

Carl Llewellyn Weschcke and Joe H. Slate, Ph.D.
℅ Llewellyn Worldwide
2143 Wooddale Drive, Dept. 978-0-7387-1893-4
Woodbury, Minnesota 55125-2989, U.S.A.

Please enclose a self-addressed stamped envelope for reply,
or $1.00 to cover costs. If outside U.S.A., enclose
international postal reply coupon.

Many of Llewellyn's authors have websites with additional information and resources. For more information, please visit our website at http://www.llewellyn.com.

PSYCHIC EMPOWERMENT
FOR EVERYONE

You Have the Power,
Learn How to Use It

CARL LLEWELLYN WESCHCKE
JOE H. SLATE, PH.D.

Llewellyn Publications
Woodbury, Minnesota

First Edition
First Printing, 2009

Cover art © Digital Vision Global Interface
Cover design by Lisa Novak
Editing by Connie Hill
Photos courtesy of Joe H. Slate
Illustration on page 31 by the Llewellyn Art Depatment

For the numerous anecdotes found in this book, either releases were obtained from the subjects at the time of the events, or the subjects' participations were with the tacit understanding that their statements might be published.

Llewellyn is a registered trademark of Llewellyn Worldwide, Ltd.

Library of Congress Cataloging-in-Publication Data

Weschcke, Carl Llewellyn, 1930–
  Psychic empowerment for everyone : you have the power, learn how to use it / Carl Llewellyn Weschcke, Joe H. Slate. — 1st ed.
      p.   cm.
  Includes bibliographical references and index.
  ISBN 978-0-7387-1893-4
  1. Psychic ability.   I. Slate, Joe H.   II. Title.
  BF1031.W418   2009
  133.8--dc22   2009034450

Llewellyn Worldwide does not participate in, endorse, or have any authority or responsibility concerning private business transactions between our authors and the public.
  All mail addressed to the author is forwarded but the publisher cannot, unless specifically instructed by the author, give out an address or phone number.
  Any Internet references contained in this work are current at publication time, but the publisher cannot guarantee that a specific location will continue to be maintained. Please refer to the publisher's website for links to authors' websites and other sources.

Llewellyn Publications
A Division of Llewellyn Worldwide, Ltd.
2143 Wooddale Drive, Dept. 978-0-7387-1893-4
Woodbury, Minnesota 55125-2989, U.S.A.
www.llewellyn.com

Printed in the United States of America

OTHER BOOKS BY JOE H. SLATE, PH.D.

Aura Energy for Health, Healing & Balance
Beyond Reincarnation
Psychic Vampires
Rejuvenation

FORTHCOMING BY CARL L. WESCHCKE AND JOE H. SLATE, PH.D.

Self Empowerment through Self Hypnosis
Self Empowerment and the Sub-Conscious Mind
Psychic Empowerment: Tools and Techniques

FORTHCOMING BY CARL L. WESCHCKE AND LOUIS CULLING

The Complete Magic Curriculum of the Secret Order G.B.G.
Dream E.S.P.
The Pristine Yi King
The Manual of Sex Magick

ABOUT THIS BOOK

What's the difference between "Psychic Phenomena" and "Psychic Empowerment?"

Yes, it may be fun and exciting to read about the strange world of the paranormal, where people talk with the dead, travel out-of-body, see at a distance, read auras, and move objects with thought alone— *but how much more exciting it should be to do it yourself!*

Yes, it may be entertaining and helpful to be in the audience in a TV show where the host or guest communicates on your behalf with the recently deceased, and answers questions about life after death and where a missing object can be found, assures you of your own spiritual immortality, and of continuing love between the worlds— *but how much more helpful it will be to do all this yourself.*

Yes, reading, listening, and watching are all easy, safe, and non-challenging ways to learn more about the paranormal world, *but how much more empowering to be doing it yourself.*

Well, you are part of it. Everyone has psychic powers, and anyone can develop psychic skills to turn those powers into ways you can live a more exciting life, ways that will provide you with helpful enhancements to all that you do and experience, and ways to give your life greater meaning and purpose. *Psychic empowerment is available to you.*

That's the difference between relating to phenomena from the outside and producing it from the inside. That's the difference between being an observer and being an active doer with intent. That's the difference between being a receiver and being a giver. *Psychic empowerment is about your own psychic skills.*

To become empowered is to have it all. To become psychically empowered is to grow in ways that bring personal benefit and spiritual attainment. Psychic empowerment expands your awareness and understanding of everything that is happening and gives you the means to participate in change. In this book the authors open your eyes to the fascinating inside view of the world and open your heart and mind to being part of that world. In this book the authors provide you with the means to become more than you are and to fulfill your life purpose. *Psychic empowerment gives your life meaning and purpose.*

Psychic Empowerment for Everyone shows that you already have psychic powers and shows you how to turn them into psychic skills that will enhance your relationships, improve your job skills, increase your self-knowledge and self-understanding, and will set you on the path of the great adventure of living more fully physically, emotionally, mentally and spiritually. The choice is yours to make.

Carl Llewellyn Weschcke

CONTENTS

FOREWORD

PSYCHIC POWERS

Most people think they know what psychic powers are: skills such as clairvoyance, reading auras, seeing the future in the cards, answering questions with a crystal ball, dowsing for water or other valuable commodities, sensing and healing health conditions, and other once-seemingly miraculous things.

Many people still think such skills are a rare gift: a talent that few are born with, one that may even be limited to people from exotic and far-off places or who have been rigidly trained since birth. Some have encountered readers at a psychic fair or amusement carnival, or consulted a professional met through referral or advertising. Some psychics have become famous and appear on talk shows, are the subject of articles, and have become book authors; their stories and the subject itself are presented in television dramas and documentaries.

Some people confuse astrology with psychic skills. Astrology is basically a technical application of astronomy and mathematics combined with thousands of years of observation of the relationship between planetary combinations and both human behavior and mundane coincidence. Some astrologers may also, unknowingly, apply their native psychic skills when working their scientific craft. It is this combination of professional or craft skills and psychic skills that make for the most successful accomplishment in any field of activity.

For myself, I will go so far as to say that I believe all success is a combination of professional training and experience in whatever profession or vocation, and psychic abilities—and that both can be developed side by side for greater personal success. You, all of us, have psychic abilities because they are a natural part of our being, but they can and should be developed for the greater fulfillment of your potential as a human being who is all of these things—physical, emotional, mental, psychic, and spiritual—all functioning in parallel.

The subject of psychic powers is now studied as *the paranormal* by scientists known as parapsychologists. Dr. Joe Slate is a parapsychologist, a practicing psychologist, the author of sixteen books in three languages, a clinical hypnotist, the founder of the International Parapsychology Research Foundation, and a retired professor from the University of Northern Alabama.

I have known Joe for more than a dozen years, as his publisher and as a friend. We are compatriots sharing interests and values, and dreams of an evolving humanity growing in mind and spirit, of individuals fulfilling their destiny of becoming more than they are by developing their psychic potentials.

I am honored that Dr. Slate has asked me to co-author this book. I told him I would only agree to this if we clearly identified him as lead author with the final say on everything I contributed. This is his book to which I am honored to contribute.

PSYCHIC POWERS, PARANORMAL POWERS, WHAT, REALLY, DO WE MEAN?

"Para" means parallel, alongside, separate but somewhere close by. Two avenues run parallel to each other: Madison Avenue in parallel with Fifth Avenue. Nowhere do they meet. But, there are cross streets that intersect with them: 32nd Street and 33rd Street, for example, providing access between them. Four streets that encompass a city block; many blocks together make a city; many cities compose a country; and many countries make the world. Today, we are becoming a global civilization wherein we are connected together through the Internet and mass communications networks, global commerce, international law and courts, global response to natural disasters, and a growing global culture of common interests in entertainment, fashion, books, spirituality, and more.

Paranormal powers are not any stranger to our world than are two avenues running parallel. We all have these psychic powers. They are innate to each and every one of us. We experience them under different names, like intuition and in dreams, and under many circumstances, such as spontaneous clairvoyance or a hunch. To develop them is not much different than taking 32nd Street to go from Madison to Fifth Avenue. Having a map and knowing where you want to go makes these parallel skills easily attainable, just as you learned mathematics and communication, in school.

Most importantly: just as learning mathematics and communications has helped you become a more competent person, so will learning to develop and utilize your psychic skills. Then you will no longer be limited to the two dimensions I've described as Madison and Fifth avenues. Instead of just moving between the two avenues by using the cross streets, you can—in a sense—move upward so that you can experience the traffic of both avenues simultaneously along with the life of the entire block. You've moved to a higher perspective and now see a more complete picture that combines the material and psychic worlds. They really are not separate worlds, but one world of many dimensions.

I'm a thinker, an observer, a philosopher, and for fifty years I've been a book publisher. I ask the big questions: *Why are we here? What is our purpose in life?* You can ask the big questions in many different contexts—You can ask: *What does God want of us?* You can ask: *What is the end goal of human evolution?* More importantly you can ask: *What is it that gives meaning to my life?*

I've looked through microscopes and telescopes, I've studied psychology and physics, I have academic degrees and I've been initiated into spiritual and religious groups, I've researched the questions, and I've meditated and addressed the questions to higher powers.

OUR LIFE PURPOSE

There is only one answer: we are here to grow, to become more than we are. Wherever you turn your vision, there is living consciousness that is growing and evolving. The process is infinite and it is slow. But, each of us has free will, and we have the ability to apply our inherited powers and our emerging skills to the challenge of accelerating personal growth.

That's what your life purpose is: to grow and to become more than you are.

And the purpose of this book is to help you develop your psychic powers to bring that very important but largely neglected area of your potential into full flower.

Some spiritual teachers tell you to ignore your psychic powers. Some also tell you to ignore the physical world. Some tell you to divest yourself of your wealth—often giving it to them. Yes, they are right if your only motivation is to have power over other people, to have more money and possessions than other people, to be better than other people. *But they are wrong to tell you not to grow in all your potentials, guided by mind as well as spirit, and becoming a more complete person.*

We all have an obligation to fulfill our potentials, to use our greater skills to help ourselves and to make a better world. Some Native Americans say we should "walk in beauty," thus leaving our bit of the world more beautiful than we found it. We have the power to function, responsibly, as co-creators in the image of our Divine Source. I believe this is what God/Goddess/Creator/Source wants of us: in essence, to become more god-like and god-filled. We are holy, which also means we must become more whole.

THE BIG SECRET

And, I'll tell you a little secret—or maybe it's a big secret—you will be happier, healthier, and more successful in whatever way you choose by developing your psychic powers. You will be a more spiritual person. You will be a more whole person. Your life will have meaning, and you will know it. You will be a citizen of the world. You will know that you live forever in a far greater universe than ever perceived through a mere physical telescope.

Yes, you will become more than you are. That's what your life purpose is. It's the journey of a lifetime.

Bon Voyage,
Carl Llewellyn Weschcke

INTRODUCTION

Part One, by Carl Llewellyn Weschcke

When Dr. Slate and I started planning this book, I suggested that it would be interesting if we each wrote half of the Introduction. Having made the suggestion, I got to write the first half. Dr. Joe Slate is a scientist and a university professor, so his part of the introduction is different than mine. I'm more a visionary and a motivator. I *want* you to develop your psychic powers. I *believe* that doing so is important to your well-being, and to the well-being of all people and the planet itself. I hope to *inspire* you to become more than you are. I want you to access 100 percent of your potential, not just the 10 percent commonly accepted as our limitation. I want you to reach out for a higher destiny, that of being filled with Divine Energy and recognition of your own life purpose. *I want you to go for it!*

LOVE IS A MANY-SPLENDORED THING

And we, each of us, are *many-dimensional beings*. There is a connection between love, the nature and structure of our being, and the development of our psychic powers.

Our physical bodies are a complex composite of bones, tissues, organs, nerves, fluids, energies, and above all, of *information packets* that instruct how each tiny cell functions, how every organ does its work, how every nerve and every vein carries energies and hormones to designated places, and how everything relates together to make a functioning and healthy body.

It is *love* that holds all the many parts together in a functional unity. Love brings people together in relationships, but it is also love that holds all the cells and organs and parts of the body together, and that holds all the many "bodies" (physical, psychic, emotional, mental, spiritual, and even extra-spiritual) together in the person each of us is. And it is love that allows us relationships with other many-dimensional beings and with our Divine origin. There is no limit to love as it is the creative force of the Cosmos.

You can give this love other names if you prefer: attraction, gravity, magnetism, nuclear force, and others, but love is something we know. We experience the power of attraction, and we experience the yearning to love. We want to receive love and we want to give love. Through love, we seek expansion, to go beyond ourselves, to reach out toward union with the beloved, and through union we go beyond present limitations.

Love Is a Many-Splendored Thing was an Academy-Award-winning 1955 film and the title of the song written for the movie, and it then became a television series running from 1967 to 1973. The meaning of the story was that love can't be limited by artificial barriers. The song says that love gives a reason to live, and that through love a man becomes a king. Motivated by love, a person—male or female—becomes more than he or she is. No matter what attribute, skill, power, or avocation we talk about, our motivation to grow and become more than we are is love. Not always the love of a man for a woman or of a woman for a man, but love is a force that attracts the object of our desire and ambition.

LOVE, GROWTH, AND WHOLENESS

What, you may ask, has love got to do with psychic development?

More than you think. But, first, let me explain: I prefer using the word "love" because we all know the experience of love. We understand the power of attraction. We know how love motivates us to reach out to embrace and incorporate the object of love into our being.

Love is what drives us toward wholeness, and wholeness is all about psychic power. Wholeness is about consciously incorporating what we already have, and developing its potential. And what we have are infinite possibilities waiting for our discovery and desire to develop them.

We all have psychic powers because they are part and parcel of the psychic body that is part of our being; but for most of us that body is outside of our conscious awareness. We don't think about anything psychic as part of a *body*, just as we don't think of emotion and feeling as part of an emotional body, we don't think of thinking and mental operations as part of a mental body, and we don't think of prayer and our spirituality as part of a spiritual body.

Nevertheless, the ancient science of occult anatomy does recognize these various bodies, although not always under the names I've given them here. Rather than using traditional occult or religious names, or the difficult Hindu names, I've chosen to describe them in the most familiar functional manner rather than to obscure things with an unfamiliar vocabulary. Even the word "occult" is obscure for many people, and for some it is associated with the scare tactics of various professionals who deliberately or ignorantly misuse the word.

THE MEANING OF "OCCULT"

Occult simply means that which is, at least temporarily, hidden from our perception. During an eclipse when the moon passes in front of the sun, this is an "occultation," simply meaning that the moon is hiding the sun from our sight. It's temporary, but unless the viewer has been educated to understand what an eclipse is, it will be very scary. Sometimes, in the distant past before there was any kind of public education, priest/astronomers would know of a coming eclipse, stir up the people with fear, and then miraculously make the sun reappear, thus making themselves powerful. *What did they really do?* They kept knowledge to themselves, hiding it from the people, and thus used their *occult* knowledge for personal power and benefit.

Hiding, suppressing, censoring, or restricting knowledge to an elite group is evil, but the so-called "occult knowledge" is not itself evil. Astronomy is not evil. The practice of medicine is not evil. Nor is astrology—the use of astronomy to forecast and better understand worldly and human events—evil. No knowledge is evil, but knowledge is always a source of power, and it is people who withhold knowledge and abuse the power it gives them who are evil.

Some of these people are well intentioned. They believe in withholding knowledge because they see ordinary people as "children," *like sheep,* unable to handle the truth. Now we see the importance of educating children to understand and handle knowledge of the world in which we all live. We educate our children so they won't be abused and manipulated by those in the know. We still protect people, adults and children, from those who abuse knowledge and power, but not by withholding knowledge.

The word "occult" has been used to describe all sorts of hidden, obscure, or not readily understood phenomena and practices. Even medical anatomy was once considered occult and as a result all sorts of errors were common.

Not many years ago, hypnotism was called occult, and was feared. Now it is commonly used in medical and psychological practices, and can safely and beneficially be used by anyone as self-hypnosis. There is nothing dangerous or evil about hypnotism—but a lack of understanding about the principles and practice of hypnosis can leave a person open to abuse. Abuse can be done not just by bad people, but by politicians, advertisers, and even your best friends who have only good intentions. Words can be used to fascinate, to arouse your emotions, and lead you to act without thought—gaining your vote, leading you to make unnecessary purchases, and even to going out on the town when you should be back at the dorm studying.

YOUR PSYCHIC POWERS HAVE BEEN HIDDEN FROM YOU

Your psychic body and powers have been hidden from you by misunderstanding and a lack of knowledge. Psychic powers have been called occult because they are so little known. Psychic powers are nearby, over on the next avenue so to speak, but until you know about them and learn to exercise them, you have not benefited from them except through occasional premonitions, hunches, dream messages, or from consultation with a professional reader of some sort.

Psychic powers are inherently yours, but you have to bring them into your consciousness to fully benefit from them.

This is where love comes in. Love, the force of attraction, is what brings about unity and wholeness. Love opens up the barriers between people and between the different bodies (or levels, or dimensions, or whatever you may prefer calling them). Loving yourself for all you can be; loving your spouse and children; loving your neighbor and your enemy. Love itself opens the doors of perception to energies, beings of different vibrations and other dimensions, and brings them into your conscious awareness so that your mind can make sense of them, your feelings will sense their values, your body's intelligence will perceive healing benefit, and your spirit will make you whole.

Aleister Crowley, a famous and very misunderstood magician and occultist of the twentieth century, said, "Love is the law, love under will."

Love is the power of attraction, love is what unifies and makes whole, and love energizes and brings joy. Love is the life-force itself and it does operate under law—the very principles of creation. "Love under will" enables you to use this energy of attraction for intended consequence. All your powers of perception, mundane and psychic, enable you to see the "larger picture" and to avoid abuse through ignorance and manipulation of your desires.

How does it all work? In this book we will explain and provide guidance to experiencing and further developing your psychic powers and the skills for applying them for practical benefit.

WHOLENESS AND YOUR PSYCHIC POWERS

You can start right now. The first step is to accept that the real and whole person you are is not confined within the skin of your physical body. Already your emotions and feelings reach out beyond those limitations; already you have psychic awareness from beyond those limitations; already your mental curiosity and learning skills go beyond those limitations; already your prayers and innate spiritual powers extend past those limitations.

If you wish, close your eyes and see your whole being in your imagination. See fields of energy extending far beyond your physical body, and see many colored wheels (chakras) and bright energy lines (meridians) between your several bodies. This is the real you, and the more you visualize this image, the more complete will be the transfers of energy and awareness between your bodies and the even greater reality beyond.

Take one more step: realize that anything you imagine is real. But the depth of that reality—the *realness* of what you create with your imagination—is limited by your knowledge of what you imagine and your imaginative skills. Let us say that in your imagination you build a recognized symbol or image that represents particular realities. The more you know about those realities and the more you train your imagination and allow your imagination to be a vehicle for all your many skills, the more power you will have to control and bring that symbol or image into *realization*.

And the more you bring the force of love into this operation, the greater will be your power.

THE SECRET OF SECRETS

There, I have just given you the "secret of secrets" for becoming successful in any manner you truly desire. You have to train these skills, and you have to increase your knowledge of what it is that you desire.

If you desire to be successful in building a particular career, it should be obvious that the more you know about everything related to that career, the better. But you can look about you and see many people who are experts in that particular field, but who remain "failures," at least by your own definition of success. What is missing is what we've been talking about here: you need to extend all your many skills from your whole being to accomplish your goal, and it is with love that you energize the operation. Love is the source of power to bring your goals into reality. Imagination is the means, and knowledge focuses energy where it is needed. *Love is the law, love under will.* Think about that, meditate on it.

Love. Law. Will. And also imagination, feelings, belief, thoughts. What are these to you? As you study this book and other books, ask yourself questions and make your own definitions, and then be ready to modify them as you gain knowledge and understanding. Don't just read—think and explore, and try these new ideas out. Do the things we recommend. Learn by doing and experiencing.

Practice makes perfect, not by rote learning but because actual practice enables you to experience, and it is experience that enables you to grow and become more than you are.

Part Two, by Joe H. Slate

Working with Carl Llewellyn Weschcke on this joint effort has been one of the most rewarding experiences of my life. I was greatly honored when he agreed to join me in this writing task, and my esteem for him increased beyond bounds as we worked together. I discovered early on that his depth of psychic knowledge was unmatched, as was his commitment to use it for the higher good. I will be forever grateful for this opportunity.

PSYCHIC EMPOWERMENT IS FOR EVERYONE.

Once empowered, you can overcome all barriers to your growth and turn even the most difficult problems into exciting new growth opportunities. You'll discover that fear, insecurity, inferiority, and doubt all yield to the empowered self. Now as never before, you can make unlimited success and happiness a reality in your life.

Knowledge is power, and paranormal knowledge is power at its peak. Paranormal knowledge is relevant mentally, physically, psychically, and spiritually—as well as culturally and globally. It has relevance even on a universal and multi-universal scale. The following statements are but a few examples of the empowerment possibilities of paranormal knowledge.

THE EMPOWERMENT POSSIBILITIES
OF PARANORMAL KNOWLEDGE

- It can expand your awareness and increase your understanding of your existence as a life-force being.

- It can unveil totally new dimensions of reality and facilitate empowering interactions with them.

- It can generate mental, physical, and spiritual attunement and balance.

- It can enrich your social interactions and promote your career success.

- It can bring you into a state of harmony with other dimensions and higher planes of power.

- It can promote your development of the skills required to achieve your personal goals.

- It can reveal the endless nature of your existence as an evolving soul.

- It can promote global peace and suggest solutions to global problems, such as reckless depletion of natural resources and disregard for threatened or endangered species.

- It can dispel the myths that are often associated with the paranormal.

YOU ARE, BY NATURE, PSYCHIC

The central theme, and title, of this book is *Psychic Empowerment for Everyone*. You are, by nature, psychic. You possess an array of psychic potentials, many of which are often expressed effortlessly or spontaneously. Others, however, exist in hidden or dormant form. They require effort not only to uncover them, but even more important, to develop them. That said, acquiring relevant knowledge and mastering programs that apply it become the overarching essentials of psychic empowerment and the focus of this book.

Equipped with knowledge and related skills, you can at last take full command of the forces—both within and beyond—that affect your life. In that empowered state, you can achieve your loftiest goals and improve the quality of your life. More specifically, you can accelerate learning, improve memory, increase creativity, solve complex problems, overcome debilitating fears, promote better health and fitness, break unwanted habits, and even slow the aging process. On a larger scale, you can contribute to the greater good and make the world a better place for present and future generations. Although some of these goals may seem at first unattainable, you will discover that they are all within your reach when you become psychically empowered.

PSYCHIC EMPOWERMENT IS CONTINUOUS GROWTH

Psychic empowerment, rather than a dormant, inactive state, is a continuous process of growth and personal fulfillment. It can activate an interaction within that promotes the full unfoldment of your personal growth potentials. It's a dynamic process that helps ensure an unshakable foundation for your personal fulfillment and success. Should that process for some reason become thwarted or blocked, atrophy and decline could set in. Although greatness is your destiny, fulfilling that destiny requires your best efforts. I firmly believe that the best is yet to come, but with one caveat: *we must do whatever we can to make it happen.* When psychically empowered, you can "dream the impossible dream" and make it a reality in your life. A major goal of this book is to inspire that all-important effort.

Psychic empowerment as presented in this book is a hopeful, optimistic concept that recognizes both the complexity of the human experience and the incomparable worth of each individual. It emphasizes the emerging self as the major determinant of individual growth and success. The limitations of heredity and the adverse effects of cultural or any other environmental influence yield to the psychically empowered self and its capacity to overcome all growth barriers. Once you become fully empowered, there exists neither space nor need for alibis. You have the power, and the responsibility, to move ahead.

THE POWER OF PERSONAL EXPERIENCE

Possibly nothing offers more convincing evidence of the paranormal than personal experience. Among the examples common to almost everyone are dreams that later unfold into reality exactly as dreamed, telepathic messages from family or friends, and psychic or "intuitive" awareness of a distant situation or condition. While recognizing the importance of personal experience, this book attempts throughout to strike a reasonable balance between subjective experience and controlled scientific research. When viewed objectively, each can add validity to the other. Both can increase our understanding of paranormal phenomena and the dynamics underlying them. In recognizing the importance of both, this book presents many accounts of personal experiences, including those of the authors, along with the results of laboratory studies conducted over several years at Athens State University in Alabama. The studies that are cited by technical report (TR) numbers are available for review at the University's library archives.

People differ and times change. Multiple forces—internal and external, conscious and subconscious—constantly interact to influence our behavior. When psychically empowered, you can take command of the complex forces that influence your life. Through the concepts and programs presented in this book, you can become the master architect of your destiny. Beginning now, you can add meaning, happiness, success, and power to your life.

CHAPTER ONE

THE PARANORMAL
New Perspectives/New Possibilities

ACCEPTED SCIENCE

It wasn't very long ago that psychic or paranormal phenomena was considered mostly as something associated with spiritualist séances, ghosts, and haunted houses. And it is only very recently (1969) that parapsychology was officially accepted as a recognized science.

The truth is, of course, that what we call paranormal has been around for a very long time—perhaps just as long as there have been human beings, and possibly even before that. *What is paranormal?* Just things that happen outside of the normal, beyond the expected, and psychic and magical skills not possessed by ordinary people. But these skills were possessed by shamans, priests, and magicians, and by the occasional "Divinely possessed" human beings who founded major religions.

Notice the use of the word "skills," not the word "powers." Everyone has psychic powers, but few have psychic skills. The goal of this book is to help you develop your psychic powers and train your psychic skills.

Both are necessary; just as it takes both a developed physical body and training in swimming to make an Olympic champion gold-medal winner, you can develop your psychic body and train your psychic skills.

For a long time, even the recognition of psychic powers was inhibited by scientific rejection and doubt that they existed, along with religious repression and the carefully nurtured general cultural belief that anything supposedly psychic was at best superstitious nonsense and at worst outright fraud.

Today, the situation is much different. Modern quantum theory has demonstrated the theoretical foundations for the paranormal, and the New Age cultural transformation has created an open mindset of acceptance of the possibilities of strange happenings and demonstrations of psychic skills.

With modern scientific acceptance, a new era has opened up.

RECOGNIZED PRACTICAL APPLICATIONS

Are there really practical applications for trained psychic skills?

The answer is yes, but you are still not going to find many employers looking for a trained clairvoyant or for astral travelers. There may be opportunities for developed psychics as entertainers and counselors, but few psychic stock-market analysts are going to be hired by Wall Street bankers (at least, not openly!).

BRAINSTORMING

So what are the recognized practical applications? First of all, success in any endeavor involves your total being, and the more successful a person is, the more likely they are drawing upon psychic skills, consciously or not, in their work. Think in terms of all the careers today that involve creativity, and that reward what we call entrepreneurship. That innovation process, sometimes called brainstorming, can be mostly attributed to drawing upon psychic skills.

There are people and products that teach the brainstorming process, and some of them, like *The Bright Idea Deck* and *Putting the Tarot to Work* (both by Mark McElroy, published by Llewellyn), use a Tarot deck to stimulate the creative processes. The Tarot lends itself very well to creative thinking because it reaches the archetypal levels of the mind that are foundational to all human experience.

THE TAROT AND ASTROLOGY

Any system that asks the user to interpret the meanings of particular symbols or combinations of symbols, or that responds to questions with answers, is a psychic system or tool. The more adept you become at using such tools, the more specific—and practical—the application can become. Some readers will use one Tarot deck for romance questions, and others for questions related to money, health, missing bits of history, lost property, etc.

The Tarot, like astrology, is both a tool and a system with a long heritage of wisdom and understanding. However, many people successfully use simple pendulums with concisely worded yes/no questions. Here, as with other psychic aids, the precision of the questions is important, but the imaginative interpretation of the answers—even of a "yes"—can be even more important. And developing questions in a progressive manner—essentially stepping stones toward a big answer—initiates a creative approach which itself is a call to the psychic faculties.

Is this a practical application? That's entirely a matter of the questions you ask, the way you ask them, and the ways you interpret the answers and then move on to new questions. As always, if you want practical answers you have to prepare practical, and sincere, questions.

It's not the paraphernalia of the system that is important, rather it is the call to the psychic powers and skills that awakens and expands the human potential to move beyond ordinary limitations. The paraphernalia is useful in opening channels to the greater consciousness and giving definition to the response.

There are many possible tools that can be used with and to augment your natural psychic powers and trained skills. Tarot and the pendulum are two of the best, but others include the use of astrology (the casting of real horoscopes, not just sun sign astrology), meditation, programming and interpretation of dreams, the famous crystal ball, the I Ching, and other divination and oracle systems. Their value will always depend upon the depth of your knowledge of them, and the appeal they have for you. None of them function independently of the operator who manipulates the tools and interprets the results. Interpretation is not a static reading of meanings for each card or symbol, but a creative and imaginative story that incorporates their generally accepted meanings.

Even astrology, which will seem to give fairly specific answers to carefully developed questions, benefits from the augmentation that comes from your psychic powers. And the more you recognize the partnership between the skillful use of these tools and your psychic powers, the richer and more beneficial will they be.

THE IMPORTANCE OF RESPECT FOR YOUR PSYCHIC POWERS

But, remember the old early-computer-era warning: *garbage in; garbage out.* It's always vital to treat your tools and your psychic powers with sincerity and respect, to always frame your questions intelligently and progressively, to treat the answers and interpretations with respect and with anticipation that they mean more than what they at first may seem to say, and to expect that some answers will progressively lead to new questions to be asked.

The inner worlds often communicate through symbols and feelings, and your feelings will often guide you toward deeper understanding. Study of the various tools, and of symbols, will add dimension to your psychic experience. The more you work with your tools, the more you understand the science and symbolism behind them, the better they will integrate with your psychic powers and skills.

Aside from such tools as the Tarot, other symbolic oracles, the pendulum, and astrology, many other divinatory tools have been used: sticks, bones, shells, playing cards, the casting of runes, throwing the I Ching, and still others. The major difference between those that involve symbol systems and those that require the manipulation of physical objects is the increased role of the fingers. Manipulating things—almost any kind of thing—with fingers and hands calls forth a particularly rich energy that imbues the manipulations with meaning.

Think of a pianist. The piano has a mechanical keyboard and each key produces a sound. But the pianist's fingers *make* the sounds. A real pianist no longer thinks in terms of musical notes; his fingers know what to do and *create* the music. A person with psychic skills can use her hands and fingers to create meaning merely by manipulating sticks and stones. It's the process of working with the fingers in expectation of receiving answers to questions that calls down meaning. It doesn't require the assignment of values to this stick, and that stick, and so on. The psychic can work with closed eyes and speak the answers, just as a blind pianist can create music.

DREAMING TRUE

Dreams are different and of particular importance because of their inner connection. An old book, now out of print, is of considerable interest. *The Conquest of Time—How You Too Can Dream True* (Harold Horwood, 1958) tells the author's story of programming his dreams to give him the names of the horses that would win in the coming races. He would write down all the horses' names for races to be run a week later, and then would review those names before falling asleep. He kept pencil and paper handy for scribbling notes first thing upon waking. Rarely did his dreams give specific names, although more than once he did see the winning horse's name, and another time heard the name shouted, waking him up with a jolt! Usually he had to deal with hints and symbols, but nevertheless he won consistently and his story in the *Sunday Pictorial* (London), January 11, 1959, listed the details and reproduced winning tickets with names, the odds, and his winnings. He was making a comfortable living.

Can Mr. Horwood's method be adapted to other situations? Yes—the method is simple, although it may not be easily adapted to every circumstance. Remember the old advice, that before you make a big decision *you should sleep on it!*

Here's a summary of Mr. Horwood's technique:

1. Study the variables in the situation (horses in the coming race).

2. Make a list of involved names or words, in no particular order. This could as easily be the names of people, stocks, locations, dates, etc.

3. Review the list each night before sleep.

4. Sleep on it.

5. Immediately upon awakening, write down details from the dreams you can remember.

6. See if you have any matches. If not, analyze your dreams to find possible connections. Look for similarities of names, symbols, signs, etc. Let the imagination loose. Choose what seems right. If it doesn't feel right, don't do it.

7. Act accordingly.

8. Record everything. Reread your journal. Study the journal to better learn the language of your dreams.

Dreams have been called "the language of the Unconscious." So are symbols. Treat your dreams with respect and pay attention to what they seem to want to tell you. Write a summary of your dreams and your interpretations, and then go back later and record your successes, any additional impressions, apparent connections between successive dreams, and connections with other psychic experiences. Remember, you are learning to build communications between your bodies and the world you live in. You are training your psychic faculties.

IS THE PARANORMAL ANOTHER WORD FOR MAGIC?

Yes it is, and no it isn't. We have to stop and consider what we mean by the word "magic" and such related words as spells, omens, witchcraft, and just about any other occult or New Age word you want to throw into the mix. If we confine the word magic to its occult usage, we can use this definition: "the use of supposed supernatural powers to make impossible things happen" (*Encarta Dictionary*, 2008). Next we have to step gingerly and clarify the meanings of these various words in the context of their usage.

"Supposed supernatural powers." Basically, we don't believe in the supposed supernatural. There's *natural*, and there's things beyond or outside our present knowledge and understanding of the extended natural universe. Just because we don't understand how something works doesn't make it *super*natural. We can argue that some things can be called occult just because their mechanism is at present hidden, or not understood, but there is nothing supernatural about it.

"To make impossible things happen" is, of course, impossible by definition of impossible. Instead, we should just say "to make things happen."

Magic is mostly defined as bringing about change in accordance with will. And, there are *magical* ways to make things happen. Modern quantum theory affirms that—at the quantum level, where things are really packets of energy, the mere act of observation changes reality, and the exercise of intention can change things in determined ways. In the sense that this action is perceived as not normal by people other than the magician, then it can be said that the paranormal is another word for magic.

Anything that is psychic can be called magical if you wish. Instead, calling the same thing *paranormal*, and studying it within the field of parapsychology changes our perception from miraculous to scientific. Speaking in terms of scientific magic is perfectly legitimate once we understand that magicians follow specific procedures to accomplish intended results.

With self-examination, you will discover a great deal of time and energy is actually occupied with idle thoughts and speculations. We can think of this as mental chatter, or even a kind of "self-gossip." But you don't empower these idle thoughts with careful planning, visualization, and intention—the will that turns thought and image into reality.

Understand the difference between mental chatter and mental action. Acting with awareness and intention along with empowerment

with energy is magical. Combining these principles with careful planning and progressive goals leads to practical success.

HEALING AND MIRACLES

Healings may occur outside standard allopathic medical practice. That
just means that the healing is not understood in terms of standard
medical practice, but it doesn't mean that the healing did not occur
and it doesn't mean that it should necessarily be called a miracle. The
Encarta dictionary defines a miracle as "an event that appears to be
contrary to the laws of nature and is regarded as an act of God."

Again, we have to say that an event that *appears* to be contrary to
natural laws should be called paranormal and studied as such. And,
what if it is "an act of God?" We should still study it within the field of
parapsychology to better understand the nature of Divine intervention and what happens to bring it about. If it is a matter of prayer,
then we need to better understand the principles of prayer, and learn
how to pray more effectively.

There should be no territorial disputes between science and religion; rather, belief is part of practice. We do things, both practical and
esoteric, in anticipation of a specific outcome. Belief is the foundation of practice. It may not be a religious belief, but we might well
ask what really makes a belief religious *only.* If we live in one great
universe, then everything is part of the whole. Whatever we do with
intention has a result. If it is not the result we anticipated, or appears
to be no result at all, then we need to study and make improvements
in our belief/understanding and our practice/application until we get
the results we want and understand how it worked.

THE PARANORMAL IS NOT
A CHALLENGE TO COMMON SENSE

Common sense comes from acceptance of observed phenomena. If
something works, it is good common sense to accept that it works
even if we don't yet understand why it works or how it works. If your
hunches prove correct, it is only common sense to pay attention to

them. If your dreams are generally presentient, it's common sense to pay attention, and at least consider them among other factors. But it is also common sense to consider such prescience along with other information when making major decisions.

Intuition and other psychic factors should be respected, but so should rational analysis of a situation. If one backs up the other, all the better; if one says yes, and the other no, then you need to take a second look, reframe the question, get a second opinion, and so on. That's just common sense. At the same time, it is learning time. Keep a journal so that you can record and analyze what you did and what happened.

Analysis, learning, and growth all come from experience and understanding.

PSYCHIC EMPOWERMENT GOES BEYOND PSYCHIC PHENOMENA

Yes, psychic phenomena, the paranormal, does include ghosts, hauntings, clairvoyance, dreaming true, seemingly miraculous healing, precognition, ESP, astral projection and out-of-body-experience, mental telepathy, psychometry, remote viewing, telekinesis, spirit communication, channeling, etc., but psychic empowerment goes far beyond these skills.

Psychic empowerment is the awakening of the whole human consciousness to its hidden and neglected powers. From another perspective, it is the empowering of the whole person, including what we call the psychic dimensions.

Our goal in this book is not to just make you a psychic, but to awaken you to everything you can be, to become more than you are, and to help you connect with the resources of your own higher consciousness.

References

Encarta Dictionary (Redmond, WA: Microsoft Corp., 2008).

Harold Horwood, *The Conquest of Time—How You Too Can Dream True* (self-published, c. 1958, printed by W. J. Fowler, London).

CHAPTER TWO

PSYCHIC PHENOMENA IN THE LABORATORY AND BEYOND

From Acceptance to Experiment and Development

DR. RHINE'S LABORATORY AT DUKE

While psychical phenomena had been the subject of serious scientific research from the mid-1800s on, it was the work of Dr. J. B. Rhine, starting in 1931 at Duke University, that moved parapsychology from the study of the incredible to the credible. Testing the psychic abilities of one person after another and showing many to have statistically significant and even dramatic results far above chance, Rhine not only proved that psychic powers were real but that they were far from rare. In 1969 the Parapsychology Association became an affiliated organization of the American Association for the Advancement of Science, providing the recognition of parapsychology as a legitimate field of scientific study and research.

Today, there are parapsychology courses at many universities and psychical research continues at an increasing number of parapsychology laboratories at universities around the world, with considerable funding from various foundations and military agencies. No one knows for sure the extent of the funding that may be *off the book* in 2008, with both government and private corporations.

There have been many claims of Pentagon funding of research into astral projection and remote viewing as well as telepathy, telekinesis, and precognition. It's about as difficult to verify these reports as it is to verify the claims that the frozen bodies of aliens from the Roswell, New Mexico UFO event are stored at Wright-Patterson Air Force Base. There are things we may never know about what goes on behind the closed doors of our military and intelligence services and those of other nations.

But these claims don't really matter to us in this book. What does count is that science does recognize psychic phenomena as real and that most people demonstrate at least minimum psychic powers. This alone is empowering, for it says that you have the power and you have the opportunity to develop this power and turn it into skills for both practical application and spiritual attainment.

Laboratory research can be designed to identify the various types of psychic phenomena and uncover the dynamics associated with them. It can formulate effective developmental programs and test the relevance of various theoretical models. It can advance the technology required to monitor the mental and physical variables associated with psychic performance. The evidence is clear: psychic phenomena exist in diverse forms, many of which can be identified and investigated in the experimental laboratory setting.

Early on, psychic research at Alabama's Athens State University (then College) became a major component of the parapsychology program under the direction of Dr. Joe H. Slate. The parapsychology program at the university has received wide recognition for the quality of its research as well as its instructional program.

The research has varied from simple classroom instructional exercises to highly controlled laboratory projects. The focus, however, was consistent: to explore the existence of psychic phenomena and uncover ways of developing the psychic potential existing in everyone. Among the topics investigated were extrasensory perception (ESP), psychokinesis (PK), altered states of consciousness, reincarnation, health and fitness, rejuvenation, pain management, learning and memory, electrophotography, and the human aura, to mention only a few.

A university laboratory can be a very controlled environment, but sometimes the most unexpected things can happen. We can relate a wonderful story told directly to Dr. Slate by a person who witnessed it firsthand. When, shortly after it was founded, members of Duke University's board of trustees visited Dr. Rhine's laboratory to observe an experiment in psychokinesis, the unexpected did happen.

In this particular experiment, an ordinary bell, placed on a table, levitated and drifted around the ceiling, and then returned to the table. One of the trustees arrogantly asserted that the experiment was suspect and, as such, did nothing to benefit the academic image of the university. With that, an unseen force ripped off the collar from the trustee's shirt and threw it to the floor!

That trustee was so distraught from this experience that he had to be helped from the room. Dr. Rhine's research program received no further criticism from the board of trustees.

The person who told the story to Dr. Slate was Dr. James E. Bathurst, then a research associate of Dr. Rhine and later Academic Dean at Athens State University.

Incidents like this are a firm reminder that we must treat paranormal phenomena with respect, for their origin and their power is our own. Our psychic power is real, although long ignored, long neglected, and often repressed. When accepted as originating in our own whole self, it is a *force*, and a force that can be developed into personal skills and magnified through people working together as a team, or in partnership, or a cohesive group.

Now we are ready to bring that power into its own, integrated into the whole and holy person that each of us is becoming.

THE PARAPSYCHOLOGY LAB
FOR DISCOVERY AND RESEARCH

Why do we do laboratory research? With statistical and experimental studies we seek to understand more about any observed phenomenon—whether the object is material, botanical, biological, astronomical, geological, or human. Or spiritual! With greater understanding, we learn more about how the phenomenon works, what its natural purpose may be, and how it relates to other natural phenomena.

But we also start the process of learning how it can be developed and adapted in possibly practical ways to benefit people. That's how science lays the foundation for technology, and then technology explores practical applications and develops beneficial products.

Imagine, for example, a device no larger than a cell phone that could provide an instant measurement of your current mental and physical state. Imagine that by simply placing your right index finger on the screen of the device, you could access in an instant a detailed assessment of your present efficiency level, to include your ability to make decisions, solve problems, and manage stress. Beyond these, imagine the capacity of the device to predict your future, identify the conditions required for your immediate and future success, and even signal physiological malfunctions that may need psychological or medical attention. Implausible though it may seem, research related to electrophotography suggests that a device with these capacities may be in the not too distant future.

Developed by the Russian scientists Semyon and Valentina Kirlian in 1939, electrophotography is a contact technique in which the object being photographed, such as a finger tip, is placed in direct contact with film set on a metal plate charged with electricity of high voltage and frequency.

While considered of minimal importance by some, the discovery of electrophotography was hailed by many parapsychologists and other scientists as "a way to see the unseeable" and "a window on the unknown," which could revolutionize our concept of self and the universe (Ostrander and Schroeder, 198). Ostrander and Schroeder concluded that the Kirlians had photographed the etheric, or energy, body and provided a new technique for "exploring the energy body of ESP" (206). The *radiation field photography* research of Moss and Johnson at UCLA appeared to corroborate the findings of the Russian scientists, thus stimulating added interest in the Kirlian technique (Moss and Johnson, 1972). According to Moss and her associates, electrophotography provided visual evidence of important *bio-energetic interactions*. Similarly, Krippner and Rubin (1974) saw the photographic recordings as a manifestation of the so-called *galaxies of life*.

Among the several electrophotographic studies conducted at Athens State University was a project funded by the U.S. Army Missile Research and Development Command (Slate, 1977) to investigate electrophotography and its potential application to the military environment. Consisting of a thirteen-month investigation, the study titled *Investigations Into Kirlian Photography* used electrophotography to record the corona discharge patterns noted around the right index fingerpad. The recorded patterns were then analyzed to determine their characteristics and prospective utilization. Figure 1 presents the experimental arrangement for obtaining the electrophotographic images.

Figure 1. Experimental Arrangement for Obtaining
Electrophotographic Images.

The study was characterized by rigorous scientific controls, careful quantification of the electrophotographic recordings, and appropriate statistical treatment of the information derived under various experimental conditions. Like earlier studies, this project offered convincing evidence of the important relevance of corona-discharge patterns obtained using electrophotography.

Here are some of the major findings of the study:

Statistical as well as visual analysis of the results showed for the first time a basically stable, but unique, corona-discharge pattern around the right index fingerpad for each of the twenty-two participants, a phenomenon labeled the individual's "electrophotographic signature." This finding suggested that the recorded images could be used for identification purposes.

Accurate fingerprints were obtained using electrophotography, a finding which could lead to an easy, clean, and readily automated method for obtaining fingerprints.

Measurable differences were observed between the recorded images for males and females, with females typically showing greater symmetry in their electrophotographic patterns as illustrated in Figure 2.

A measurable difference was observed between the relaxed state and the "no treatment," or normal, state for each of twelve participants, with the relaxed state showing a decrease in pattern intensity, a finding suggesting possible stress-monitoring applications.

Statistical correlations for ten subjects were obtained between the electrophotographic recordings and certain standardized test results for various psychological states, including anxiety and depression, a finding that suggested possible psycho-diagnostic applications.

The results of this research led to the formulation of an automated electrophotographic image apparatus capable of recording and correlating electrophotographic images of the fingerpad for a variety of applications. After an image is obtained and stored in an image digitizer, the digitized image becomes computer readable and is compared to the standard image for a given person, printing out any pertinent information such as a positive or negative identification or any change noticed from the subject's standard or normal state.

*Figure 2. Typical Electrophotographic
Images for Male (left) versus Female (right).*

An advanced system for the continuous monitoring of an individual's physical and emotional state would require more extensive research, but could conceivably be developed utilizing a modified electrophotographic recording system (such as a wristband, ear-tab, or even an implanted device) that would detect any changes in the stability or other emotional traits of the individual.

Based on this study, the electrophotographic technique appears to have application in detecting mental states and thought processes for which the corresponding physiological processes are at present either unknown or sufficiently minimal as to be considered nonsignificant. It is suggested that electrophotography, pending further research, may have application as a sensitive detector of motives or intents, a more direct, efficient, and sophisticated type of lie detector that is not dependent on physiological processes.

The research findings of this project suggest possible applications for security purposes, pending further investigations, some of which are now underway. For example, more extensive research may show that simple security mechanisms could be designed to respond only to the touch of selected personnel through an *electrophotographic response system* or ERS. Vehicles as well as residential and industrial facilities could conceivably be designed and equipped so that accessibility is automatically and completely controlled.

It seems plausible that future research could result in the development of an advanced electrophotographic unit no larger than a cell phone, or even much smaller, to provide instant analysis of an individual's mental and physical state. Such a unit could be activated on demand by the individual to indicate present levels of intellectual efficiency, emotional stability, and competency indexes related to such tasks as decision making, problem solving, and planning. The implications are profound and could even include predictions (and cautions) based on current corona-discharge activity. Routine use of such a unit could become a good way to start your day.

We have moved beyond the confirmation of psychic phenomena as genuine to an increasing understanding of how they are integrated in the whole-body experience and how the mechanisms can be adapted to numerous practical applications.

THE LAB AS VALIDATION

Efforts to validate psychic phenomena can take several forms. Among the possibilities are carefully designed lab studies that test psychic observations, theories, and claims originating outside the lab setting. For phenomena already investigated in the laboratory setting, common validation strategies include replication studies by other investigators.

In some instances, validation efforts can take the form of follow-on studies that take the research findings of earlier projects to a new level. That strategy was used in a follow-on study conducted at Athens State University in an effort to further determine the relevance of electrophotography to a host of physical, psychological, and parapsychological variables (Slate, 1985). The six-month laboratory study titled *The Kirlian Connection: New Discoveries in Electrophotography*, funded by the Parapsychology Foundation of New York, was conducted in five phases under rigorously controlled laboratory conditions. A major focus of the study was on altered states of consciousness and the capacity of electrophotography to monitor those states. Such a finding could have important implications for identifying

Figure 3. Electrophotographs for No-treatment (left)
versus Relaxation (right).

various altered states and developing appropriate training strategies related to them. Here are some of the major findings of this study:

Repeated photographic recordings of the right index fingerpad for twenty subjects over an eight-week period revealed significant stability of pattern characteristics when finger orientation and pressure applied between the finger and film were held constant.

Electrophotographic recordings obtained during the no-treatment, or normal, state and those obtained during relaxation showed a significant difference, with the relaxation recordings typically showing a marked decrease in corona-discharge activity for the twenty subjects participating in this phase of the study (Figure 3).

Consistent with previous research, this finding suggests possible application of electrophotography in monitoring relaxation states and training in relaxation techniques.

Marked differences were noted between the no-treatment electrophotographs and certain altered states to include hypnosis, age regression to childhood, and the past-life regression state. For each of fifteen subjects participating in this phase, a decrease in corona-discharge activity was noted for hypnosis and a further decrease was noted for age regression to childhood, a phenomenon called *image decline effect*. In the past-life regression state, the recordings showed an intensity increase beyond that for the normal state, a phenomenon called *past-life illumination* (Figure 4).

A unique pattern called the *broken-corona effect* was characteristic of electrophotographs taken during the out-of-body state for ten subjects,

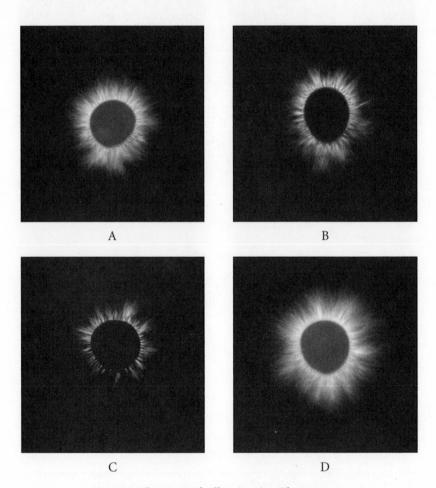

Figure 4. The Past-Life Illumination Phenomenon.
Photographs for (a) no-treatment, (b) hypnosis,
(c) age regression to childhood, and (d) past-life regression.

each of whom reported having had previous out-of-body experiences (Figure 5).

Figure 5. The Broken Corona Effect,
an effect observed for the out-of-body state.

Several methods for quantifying the corona discharge images were identified. One means involved a model designed to quantify the light reflected or transmitted by the electrophotograph (Figure 6).

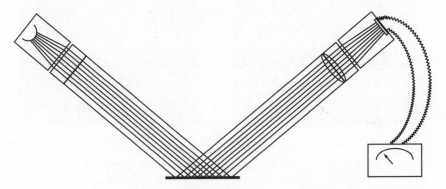

Figure 6. Theoretical Model for Quantifying the Kirlian Electro-photograph.

The findings of this study suggested that all of the altered states investigated—hypnosis, age regression to childhood, past-life regression, and out-of-body—are *separate and distinct states of consciousness*. These observed effects suggest a highly useful application of electrophotography toward monitoring altered states and evaluating training methods. In other words, many of our psychic skills have specific correlations to altered states, and techniques to attain these specific states can also be used to access these skills.

Among the interesting findings of this study was the nature of the past-life experiences reported by subjects during the past life regression state. Based on the electrophotographs as well as their own reports, all fifteen subjects participating in this phase of the project successfully experienced the past-life regression state. Their experiences during that state were typically characterized by normal, everyday activities rather than intense, life-changing heroic happenings. Here are a few examples:

Female, age 43: I'm standing on a high, windswept hill. The wind is blowing very strongly and I feel a mist of rain on my face. Looking below, I see a grassy meadow with animals grazing in the distance. The surrounding country has very high hills or mountains with high cliff-like structures. I have never traveled far from this place. Scotland has always been my home.

Male, age 25: There is a large gathering of people to participate in a festive religious holiday. The Pharaoh is here; also guards, priests, slaves, and aristocrats. I am one of the priests of the god Osiris. I am dressed in a long robe, midnight blue with gold trim, and a headdress with a gold, sun-like object on top.

Male, age 22: I am a very old man, dressed in a long white, one-piece garment. The buildings are huge spires rising to very great heights. The city, including its corridors, is made of a clear glass-like material. There exists here a highly advanced technology. There are ways of altering matter and energy as well as life processes. The old remain young—they grow older but not old, until it is time to go. There is no disease, mentally or physically. Sound channels, or energy channels, exist in which thought takes a crystal-like form. These are used as energy sources, mainly for healing. There are ways of communicating thought without sound.

This study illustrated the effectiveness of follow-on research to validate the findings of earlier studies while acquiring additional insight and uncovering new applications.

THE LAB AS EXPERIMENTAL

Nothing succeeds like success. It's a familiar concept, and there's plenty of evidence to support it. Studies of college students, for instance, have consistently shown that the single best predictor of future success is recent past success. Studies of success in business have repeatedly shown similar results, thus raising the question: Could past success literally program individuals and organizations alike for future success, possibly by generating a powerful self-fulfilling prophecy or expectancy effect? Given that possibility, could intervention strategies be designed to increase the probability of success? The study that follows was designed to investigate these possibilities.

While past studies of psychic phenomena often focused on the existence and explanations of the paranormal experience, the direction of present research has shifted to include ways of developing our psychic potentials and using them to achieve our personal goals. Such practical applications as achieving career success, finding happiness, solving personal problems, resolving conflicts, improving memory, and working more effectively with people are all now within the scope of psychic research in the laboratory setting.

Although researching these important areas may demand controlled lab conditions, it does not always require elaborate experimental equipment. In a recent study sponsored by the International Parapsychology Research Foundation (TR-76), the only materials required were a twenty-item list of words and sixty pens and note pads. The study was designed to investigate the effects of certain pre-test conditions on future learning and retention.

A group of sixty undergraduate students consisting of thirty-four females and twenty-six males volunteered for the study. The age range of the subjects was seventeen through twenty-nine years. The subjects were randomly divided into three groups of twenty subjects each. Each group was seated comfortably in a quiet classroom setting and each subject was provided a pen and writing pad. The task of the three groups was to recall as many words as possible from a list of twenty words presented verbally by a research technician.

Group A, the control group, received no experimental treatment and was instructed by a research technician as follows: "The purpose of this experiment is to test your memory for words presented to you verbally. You will be presented verbally a list of twenty words. Your task will be to recall as many of the words as possible and record them on the note pad provided. You will be allowed ten minutes to record the words." The technician then presented verbally the twenty-item list.

The experimental Group B was presented the same pre-test instructions but with the addition of the following exercise: "Take a few moments now to settle back, relax, and picture a very relaxing scene—perhaps a mountain stream, a clear blue sky with a fluffy white cloud drifting slowly across it, or a still moonlit lake. You will be at your peak in your ability to recall the following list of words." The technician then presented verbally the twenty-item list.

Experimental Group C participated in the same experimental procedure as Group B but with the addition of a post-procedure cue as follows: "You can at any moment increase your ability to recall by simply touching your forehead with the fingertips of either hand." The technician then presented verbally the twenty-item list.

Statistical analysis of the results revealed that the two experimental groups B and C performed at a higher average percentage recall level for all words in the list, regardless of the position of the word, when compared with the control group A. Experimental Group C, which received the post-procedure cue, however, performed at a significantly higher level than Group B, which received no cue. Furthermore, the serial position effect, or the tendency to remember items presented near the beginning and end of a series with greater frequency than items in the middle, was less pronounced for the two experimental groups when compared with the control group.

These conclusions suggest that procedures designed to trigger certain mental functions and generate a positive expectation of success could significantly accelerate learning and retention while minimizing such inhibitors as the serial position effect. More research is needed to further identify the conditions that promote success, whether in learning situations or other settings, by activating relevant mental functions, including the effects of expectation on achievement.

Here we have described a relatively simple experiment that leads to a remarkably powerful conclusion: *Nothing succeeds like a powerful expectation of success.* It is this that mobilizes not only our mental resources but calls upon our psychic resources in order to accomplish well-established goals.

OUT-OF-BODY EXPERIENCES IN THE LAB

The lab as experiential can include investigations of such phenomena as out-of-body experiences during which experimental subjects travel out of body to experience distant realities. To investigate that application, a study was designed in which ten volunteer subjects who had completed a college-level course on astral projection and had at least one reported experience in out-of-body travel attempted to travel out of body under controlled lab conditions to view a painting situated on an easel in the third floor art studio of another campus building (TR-444). Prior to the experimental session and the placement of the painting on the easel, the subjects were escorted by a lab technician to the studio to view the easel, already positioned but without the painting. The identity of the painting to be later placed on the easel by another technician was known only to that technician, who was not present or otherwise involved in the study. The painting consisted of three essential elements: a rider on horseback in a thunderstorm.

Since previous research had indicated the usefulness of electro-photography in identifying the out-of-body state through the broken-corona effect, this study provided a situation in which the subject rested in a reclining position with the right index finger situated comfortably in the electrophotographic apparatus, an arrangement that permitted periodic recordings of the corona-discharge patterns for the duration of the session. Once the subject was resting comfortably with the finger properly positioned in the electrophotographic device, the following instructions were presented:

"In this experiment, your task is to leave your body and view a painting on an easel situated at the center of the art studio in Mc-Candless Hall. When you return to your body, you will be asked to describe the essential features of the painting. Let yourself now become more and more comfortable and relaxed. As you relax your body, you are at complete peace, confident, and secure. You are in complete control, safe and secure as you prepare to leave your body. Upon leaving your body, you will be free to return at any moment by simply deciding to do so. You will now be given plenty of time to leave your body, using whatever strategy you prefer, including those you have used before. Upon traveling to the art studio and viewing the painting, you will let yourself return to your body with comfort and ease."

With the exception of one subject, the electrophotographic recordings indicated a successful out-of-body state. While the unsuccessful subject was unable to identify any of the painting's three essential elements, the remaining nine subjects whose electrophotography clearly showed the broken-corona effect experienced varying degrees of success in identifying the painting's essential elements. Three identified the painting's three essential elements, four identified two of the paintings essential elements, and two identified one of the painting's essential elements.

Although it can be argued that the results of this experiment could have been influenced by factors other than out-of-body travel, such as clairvoyance, the successful subjects described the experience as distinctly unlike clairvoyance, and attributed their success to out-of-body travel.

This study illustrated the lab as experiential while demonstrating the relevance of laboratory research that applies concepts and technology generated by previous studies. Gaining greater understanding of the measurable electrical discharge phenomenon will further enable the development of specific techniques for out-of-body travel.

THE LAB AS DEVELOPMENTAL

In a two-year program called the Alpha Project sponsored by the International Parapsychology Research Foundation, the conditions and procedures conducive to wellness and well-being were studied at Athens State University (TR-401A).

Thirty subjects from ages seventeen to sixty-one years volunteered for the project. A complete medical examination and a battery of psychological tests, including personality and adjustment measurements, were administered for all participants. The diagnosed conditions of participants in the program included chronic pain, tension headaches, obesity, depression, chronic fatigue, and anxiety disorders.

Each participant in the program was instructed in a variety of self-empowering techniques including cognitive relaxation, guided imagery, biofeedback, and meditation, all designed to illustrate the capacity of mental functions to influence physiology.

Specific techniques related to the subject's condition and goals were formulated with their participation, and regular practice sessions, both individual and group, were conducted in a controlled lab setting for the duration of the project. Periodic progress assessments were obtained for each subject for the duration of the project.

Of the thirty volunteer participants, twenty-four remained in the program for a sufficient period to determine the program's effectiveness. Based on self-reports of participants as well as objective assessments, twenty of the twenty-four subjects experienced marked improvement, whereas the remaining four experienced moderate or temporary improvement.

Taken together, the results of this study suggest several interesting developmental possibilities related to the laboratory experience. For this experiment, the lab became a developmental center where workable strategies were formulated and tailored to meet the mental and physical needs of participants. Beyond that, the lab provided a setting for evaluating the progress of individual subjects as well as the overall effectiveness of the program.

At the end of the two-year Alpha Project, a six-month pain-manage-ment program called the Holistic Adventure was initiated (TR-401B). The program consisted of four major components: meditation, relaxation training, self-hypnosis, and biofeedback training, all designed to empower chronic pain patients with effective pain management strategies. All subjects participating in the study were referred by their personal physicians who monitored their medical conditions through periodic examinations for the duration of the project.

Among the techniques developed for use with the project was a two-part relaxation approach called the *Therapeutic Exchange and Pain Confrontation Approach*. Part I of the approach used therapeutic relaxation to alleviate pain by replacing it with relaxation, whereas Part II used confrontation to extinguish any residual discomfort. Both parts reject ownership of pain. Here's the two-part approach, each self-administered in a quiet setting free of distractions:

THERAPEUTIC EXCHANGE
AND PAIN CONFRONTATION

Part I. Therapeutic Exchange

"As I absorb soothing relaxation throughout my body, I am beginning to release all tension and anxiety. As I picture myself in my favorite surroundings, relaxation is flowing throughout my body. Pain is now being replaced with relaxation. Soothing relaxation is soaking into my body tissue, joints, and tendons, easing the pain away. I can now relax and enjoy life."

Part II. Pain Confrontation

"I have decided no longer to be a victim of pain. I now disown it, and I am determined to defeat it. As I approach the area of pain, I am confident of my ability to control it. I will not be intimidated by it. All the resources I need to manage pain are now at my disposal. I am now in charge of it. Having mastered pain, I can now focus on other goals."

The approach included the use of post-procedure suggestions that varied among patients as tools for managing pain. Examples included recalling a specific image or term, stroking the ear lobe, joining the tips of the fingers, or simply lifting a toe as a means of activating inner pain-management resources.

Self-ratings of the approach, along with the results of periodic medical evaluations, revealed moderate to significant reductions in pain. All participants reported greater confidence in their ability to manage pain.

What does pain management have to do with psychic empowerment? Once again, we are demonstrating the use of goal setting to call upon all the resources of the whole person. When we no longer limit those resources to the physical body and material setting, the whole person can respond, sometimes with remarkable results.

BEYOND THE LAB

If you've had a profound psychic experience—and most of us have—you may have questioned not only its significance but also the probability of similar experiences among people in general. To investigate that concern, students enrolled in experimental parapsychology at Athens State University conducted a survey of 500 volunteer undergraduate students (TR-500). The age range for participants of the survey was seventeen to sixty-three years. Sixty-eight percent of the respondents were females. In conducting the study, a deliberate attempt was made to present the questionnaire in a psychological rather than a parapsychological context in an effort to promote unbiased responses among respondents who might tend to reject experiences if perceived as psychic. Here are some of the results of the study:

A total of 483 respondents to the survey reported at least one experience of knowing, for no apparent reason, what another person was thinking (telepathy).

A total of 467 respondents reported at least one experience of knowing, for no apparent reason, what was about to happen or what was going to happen at some point in the future (precognition).

A total of 383 respondents reported having had a dream experience that predicted a future event.

A total of 181 respondents reported having known, for no apparent reason, about situations or events happening elsewhere (clairvoyance).

For this population, the findings of this survey suggested that the distribution of the frequency of psychic experiences, whether telepathy, precognition, or clairvoyance, tended to approximate the normal curve.

Here are a few examples of additional studies conducted under the auspices of the International Parapsychology Research Foundation, several of which were led by psychology students:

- Reincarnation: Exploring past lives and life between lives (TR-302).
- Health and Fitness: Developing practical, step-by-step strategies that promote better health and fitness (TR-198).
- Rejuvenation: How to slow the aging process, and in some instances, reverse it (TR-111).
- Hypnosis and Self-hypnosis: Activating your subconscious powers (TR-211).
- Dowsing: You can do it too (TR-213).
- Extrasensory Perception (ESP): How to uncover and activate clairvoyance, telepathy, and precognition (TR-212).
- Psychic Vampires: Real or imagined? (TR-333).
- The Human Aura: How to see it, interpret it, and change it (TR-400).
- Psychokinesis: Using the power of the mind to influence external and internal conditions (TR-377).
- Apparitions: Case studies (TR-313).

- The Power of Motivation, Imagery, and Emotion: Goal-directed strategies for getting what you want (TR-444).

The detailed technical reports for each of the above studies are available for inspection at the Athens State University Library Archives.

RESEARCH TO PROMOTE PERSONAL EMPOWERMENT

Research is essential to our understanding of the unexplained. It can identify the many different forms of psychic phenomena, uncover the underlying dynamics associated with them, and formulate programs that facilitate their development and application. Research can promote our personal empowerment and add quality to our lives.

We can at last conclude with confidence: *Psychic empowerment is possible for everyone.* What we can't do, as yet, is ascertain how many people will understand the personal value of developing their own psychic skills, and then undertake that development.

Motivation for growth and development of personal skills beyond those with purely vocational value is a challenge to all of us who believe in the continuing evolution of the human as individual and species. This is even more true for those of us who see such personal growth as essential to the resolution of the challenges to our global civilization and the health of the planet itself.

All we can do is to encourage each reader of this book to undertake the program of psychic empowerment, and then to encourage others to do so as well. That way you become an agent of change, an evangelist for psychic empowerment, and you demonstrate your care for all humanity and our planetary home.

References

Harold Horwood, *The Conquest of Time—How You Too Can Dream True* (self-published, c. 1958).

S. Krippner and D. Rubin, *The Kirlian Aura—Photographing the Galaxies of Life* (Garden City, NJ: Anchor Press, 1974).

T. Moss and K. Johnson. "Radiation Field Photography" (*Psychic*, 3, 50–54, 1972).

Mark McElroy, *The Bright Idea Deck* (Woodbury, MN: Llewellyn Publishing, 2005).

———. *Putting the Tarot to Work* (Woodbury, MN: Llewellyn Publishing, 2004).

S. Ostrander and L. Schroeder, *Psychic Discoveries Behind the Iron Curtain* (Englewood Cliffs, NJ: Prentice-Hall, 1970).

J. H. Slate, "Investigations into Kirlian Photography" (Technical Report, U.S. Army Missile Research & Development Command, Redstone Arsenal, AL, 1977).

J. H. Slate, "The Kirlian Connection: New Discoveries in Electrophotography" (Technical Report, The Parapsychology Foundation, New York, 1985).

Technical Reports

TR-76 The Expectancy Effect
TR-401A The Alpha Project
TR-401B The Holistic Adventure
TR-444 Out-of-Body Travel
TR-500 Student Survey—Exploring Cognitive Functions

CHAPTER THREE

BECOMING PSYCHICALLY EMPOWERED
Strategies for Success

WHAT DO WE MEAN BY THE WORD "SUCCESS"?

We cannot stress enough that psychic empowerment is about *you*! And psychic empowerment is *self*-empowerment. And while psychic self-empowerment does relate to your overall spiritual growth and attainment, the real applications are to the "here and now"—those real practical problems of everyday living. Everything you do will be enhanced by your psychic self-empowerment, and every problem you encounter will be more easily resolved by your psychic self-empowerment.

The most important word we can use to describe these practical benefits is SUCCESS! Did you notice that not only did we capitalize the word, but we ended the sentence with an exclamation mark? That's because we want to emphasize the importance of true *personal* success because it is not just about money but about your increased ability to realize all that is important to you, whether as a parent, a student, an ordinary adult, a lover, a homemaker, a hobbyist, a blue-collar worker, a white-collar worker, a crafts person, a sports professional, an entertainer, a corner-office executive, a public servant, or a waitperson. Through psychic empowerment you will be more successful in all you do.

The word, "success," is used extensively in business. Business needs to be successful, to grow in sales and profits so that it can constantly reinvest in new equipment, new products, innovative processes, and in new marketing concepts in this rapidly changing world. Old markets and old products have their day, then new products look for new markets, and new markets call for new products.

Technology has changed the ways of industry and commerce in the passage of a single generation. Technology has opened new opportunities in business and in individual careers. Even more, technology has changed lifestyles, has opened new opportunities for home work and home education, and empowered women to *have it all*. More and more, we can say: *Everyone can have it all as they learn to control their own reality.*

Primarily, when we speak of success, we are thinking in personal terms, and that is our concern in this chapter. When relating it to a *group* of any kind, the principles are similar, but the technique must include creating what has been called a "group mind." We can discuss that another time.

THE IMPORTANCE OF BIG GOALS AND MINI-GOALS

Success is the accomplishment of your goals. But one of the great secrets of success is to develop a progressive set of mini-goals, like steps along the path to your ultimate goal. Another of the great secrets is to carefully define your ultimate goal so that the steps towards the ultimate are logical, practical and sensible, and always connected to the ultimate goal. Don't think that success just means great wealth, for example, or high political office. How will you get there? What are the logical steps toward that goal, starting with where you are now?

This is very important: you must start with what your immediate options are. Recognize your limitations and your opportunities. Overcome the limitations and exploit the opportunities and then move on to the next step and repeat the process. Maybe it doesn't sound magical or like an application of psychic skill, but it is if you make it so. No matter who you are, you will not be able "to leap over tall buildings in a single bound" like Superman, but you can learn to use the elevator instead of those long stairways. Developing your psychic skills is like using the elevator.

Yes, you might hope to win the big lottery, and perhaps developing your psychic powers will help you choose the winning ticket, but the odds are tremendously against you. Your psychic power is limited when applied against great odds. Instead, learn to take advantage of odds in your favor—like swimming with the tide rather than against it. The chances of success become greater when your goals are more realistic and your starting point is practical and within reach.

Let's say you want to be a successful author. What are some of the logical steps to fulfilling your dream? Define your goals—what kind of books do you want to write? Fiction. What kind of fiction? Romance fiction. What kind of romance fiction? And so on. Clarify your goals by breaking them down into details. It doesn't mean you can't modify your goals later, because you can. That's one of the other advantages of breaking it down into steps, because with each step you can move on to alternative pathways even as your end goal remains the same. You might decide that you really want to write vampire romance fiction, and then you might decide that your lead character should be a beautiful female vampire.

Start asking and answering questions about your goals and the steps you take. How did the character become a vampire? Did it run in the family? Did her vampire lover make her into a vampire? Did she choose to become a vampire? How old was she? What was the situation? Where did it happen? What happened next? These details help define your goals and start the process of involving your psychic powers.

What you are doing is outlining the steps toward your big goal with smaller ones and becoming specific about your goal. Some teachers will tell you not to be too specific, but what they really mean is not to limit yourself, but instead be prepared to make minor changes as you move along, and even changes in your ultimate goal. There is a story about a relatively famous metaphysical writer whose dream was to have a Rolls Royce automobile. He eventually got the car—an old wreck, up on blocks, unable to run. He got what he asked for because he never clearly defined the goal. But he learned a valuable lesson for us all. *Be careful what you wish for!*

Asking yourself questions, and answering those questions, is one way to involve all your powers and skills. Remember: you are a whole entity of physical, emotional, psychic, mental, and spiritual bodies. Asking yourself searching questions is one very easy technique to call upon all your powers.

Step back for a moment. Are you equipped to be a writer? Can you write adequately? Can you type? Can you use a computer? Do you have a computer and do you have a word processing program, like Microsoft Word? Have you taken writing courses? Do you know how to market your manuscript? Who are the publishers most suited to publish your manuscript? Have you gone on-line to look for your prospective publishers' author guidelines? Do you understand the copyright law and how to protect your manuscript?

(By the way, one common error that would-be writers make is to think that they can protect their ideas. The answer is basically no. Nor can you protect the title.)

Yes, you can dream about your great goal, but don't be a dreamer about accomplishing that goal! You need to know two things: (1) You can't get to the other side of a river unless you have the means to do so—a boat, a bridge, a suspension cable, wings, an air vehicle, etc. The means of getting there from here are the mini-goals that you must not neglect. (2) The work of reaching your goal should become as much pleasure as actually getting there. That work is your career. Your means of reaching your goal are the little steps, or little goals, along the way. In the example of crossing the river, perhaps your logical means is a canoe. Become a good canoe paddler and enjoy canoeing. If your goal is to be an author, learn to enjoy every step along the way: enjoy your computer, enjoy the time you spend writing, enjoy your research, etc., and then enjoy the steps involved with your book's promotion.

Being successful means that you should enjoy every step of the process as well as the accomplishment.

WHAT ABOUT PSYCHIC POWER?

Exactly! Breaking everything down into these logical steps and attainable goals awakens your psychic powers to give you specific answers to the questions you ask—not the vague answers often heard when you go to a professional psychic and ask vague questions. Pretend again that you are a writer, and you're not sure of the next step in your book: ask your psychic self the question before you go to sleep, or go into deep meditation; you will get the answer you're looking for. If not, then reframe the question or realize you asked the wrong question and need to take a look at the particular angle you're working on.

You will learn more specific techniques in this book, but because many people have vague ideas about psychic matters, it's important to clarify that applying psychic powers to practical matters requires a common sense approach. There is nothing magical or fantastical about working with your psychic powers any more than there is about using math skills, accounting skills, and word skills. Skills of any kind require development and exercise.

And, please accept that when you decide to develop your psychic powers as partners in your success program, you're going to do some work. It's just as sensible as realizing that the ability to balance your checkbook does not mean you're qualified to be an accountant. Or that you can become an Olympic gold medal swimmer without a lot of work—step-by-step progressing through smaller goals, one after another. In this regard, developing your psychic powers and your psychic skills is no different than physical-body or mental-body accomplishments.

Psychic empowerment will add to your enjoyment of life as well as your success in life. Think of the person who is color-blind or deaf, and think how glorious it would be for that person to gain color vision and the ability to hear. Your psychic empowerment adds to every part of your life because it broadens your sensory powers as well as your intentional ones. Food will taste better with a greater variety of flavors; your romantic and sex lives will be enriched through your expanded and deepened perceptions; your enjoyment of music will become more dimensional. And you will love more. Because you are becoming more than you are, expanding beyond old limitations, you will enjoy your life more, your work more, your family more.

In becoming more through your expanding psychic powers, you have more capacity for success in all you do.

BECOMING PSYCHICALLY EMPOWERED THROUGH DIRECT EXPERIENCE

Even though you are going to learn to develop your psychic powers and skills in this book, simply being aware of psychic experiences and recognizing them for what they are starts you on the path to being psychically empowered.

As noted in the introduction, psychic powers are inherently part of your total being, but you have to bring them into your awareness to fully benefit from them. Things happen: you dream of things that later happen; you have hunches that turn out correct; you respond to feelings that tell you not to make a certain trip and later hear of an accident that would have involved you; you sense bad vibes about a certain person and later learn he's a crook. No matter whether you acknowledge it as intuition or just shrug it off as coincidence, it is real. The difference is that in acknowledging it you strengthen it and become more open to it. You open the doors of perception.

There's an old story in which, whether historically true or not, the principle has validity. The story says that when the first Spaniards arrived by ship off the coast of Patagonia, and rowed ashore in a little boat, the natives saw the Spaniards suddenly emerge miraculously from the sea because—having no experience of sailing ships—*they could not see the Spanish galleons anchored off shore.* Having no prior image of such ships, their minds could not perceive them. They could not be real because their prior experience had no place for them. The more you recognize your psychic impressions, the more broadly you will experience them.

RECOGNIZING YOUR PSYCHIC POWERS

We all have psychic experiences, but many happen below our conscious awareness, or—worse—are rejected by the conscious mind as impossible or meaningless. Instead, acknowledge them and pay attention to their possible meaning. A good idea is to start a psychic journal, like a dream journal, and record your hunches and premonitions, then look back and make note of what did happen. Even if the event that follows is not exactly what your premonition, or dream, indicated, make note of the similarities and the differences. *You are educating your psychic mode of communication.*

A very interesting book was published long ago, *An Experiment in Depth,* by P. W. Martin. The point Martin made was that most dreams seem to be mainly nonsense—sort of happening by themselves, but when you start paying attention to your dreams, recording them, *they start paying attention to you!* The dream of one night may repeat the next night, but go further, and eventually tell a complete story that is meaningful to you and may be an important guide to you.

What you are doing is learning to communicate. Wives sometimes complain about their husbands, "He never really listens to me." Husbands: *Learn to listen to your wife!* Open the communication between the two of you, and not only will you strengthen your relationship, but you may find that through the very act of listening the communications will become more meaningful. Everything is about communication, and you are expanding the communications between your bodies and your communications with the greater cosmos in which we have our being. *Communicating is always a two-way process—like asking yourself questions and giving back the answers yourself.*

It is not that your psychic powers are asleep, but that your lines of communication are being ignored. Remember that you are a greater person than the one confined inside the skin of your physical body, and that you *are becoming more than you are.* As you learn to listen, learn to ask questions and extend your awareness to include psychic impressions. After all, you can't expect to see if you have your eyes closed and you can't expect to hear unless you're alert to sounds.

THE ROLE OF COINCIDENCE

Some will say there are no coincidences, and the growing field of quantum theory *and* the old occult sciences agree: Like the old song says,

Ezekiel cried, "Dem dry bones!"
Ezekiel cried, "Dem dry bones!"
Ezekiel cried, "Dem dry bones!"
"Oh, hear the word of the Lord."

The toe bone connected to the foot bone,
The foot bone connected to the heel bone,
The heel bone connected to the leg bone,
The leg bone connected to the knee bone,
The knee bone connected to the thigh bone,
The thigh bone connected to the back bone,
The back bone connected to the neck bone,
The neck bone connected to the head bone,
Oh, hear the word of the Lord!

Dem bones, dem bones, gonna walk aroun'
Dem bones, dem bones, gonna walk aroun'
Dem bones, dem bones, gonna walk aroun'
Oh, hear the word of the Lord.

The head bone connected to the neck bone,
The neck bone connected to the back bone,
The back bone connected to the thigh bone,
The thigh bone connected to the knee bone,
The knee bone connected to the leg bone,
The leg bone connected to the heel bone,
The heel bone connected to the foot bone,
The foot bone connected to the toe bone,
Oh, hear the word of the Lord!

This is an old African-American folk song. Date and Author unknown (according to www.kididdles.com there is no known copyright and no known author).

Remember that song? *Dry Bones*—a great African-American spiritual that teaches that everything is connected, and that every connection has a deeper message. Learn to listen, recognize the connections, and you'll hear the "word of the Lord." Realization of the connections is one thing, but *you still have to listen, pay attention, and give respect to your growing psychic powers in order to hear the "word."*

That doesn't mean you should run off and invest your savings in the stock market or go gambling in Las Vegas on a hunch. You still have to learn the language of your subconscious and train the channels of communication. Don't be in too much of a hurry, and never arrogantly assume you know it all.

Coincidences are sometimes specific communications, but more often what seems to be a coincidence is a subconscious process in which your psychic self calls something to your attention that has meaning in relation to your current needs. It's the old story of letting the Bible fall open to a page and then—with eyes closed—pointing your finger to a passage and then reading it for the meaning in relation to your question. There are mechanisms at work, employed by your whole being, which has connections to the outer world, to make meaningful communications in response to your *sincere* questions. Sincerity in this context is important—unless you treat the psychic world with respect, it won't respect you. Instead, it can turn trickster. It's not the nature of the psychic world, it's your failure to treat these communications with at least as much respect as you give to your physical senses.

APPLICATIONS OF YOUR PSYCHIC POWERS

The application potentials for your psychic powers are endless. Some will depend upon your natural aptitude; others on your needs.

Think of your eyesight. When you were an infant, you had eyesight but at first you couldn't focus—scientists believe that newborn babies only perceive shadows. But as you grow older and you experience more and more, what you see takes on meaning. At certain points you recognize objects, then colors, and then words. You will be able to read rudimentary words, and then short sentences. Eventually you will be able to read a book.

Your psychic powers mature in much the same way, through experience and trial and error.

WHAT KIND OF APPLICATIONS?

What do you want to do? As a child, you decided you wanted to read a book, and eventually you learned to read books. In most cases, someone helped guide your development. The psychic world is similar.

You can have psychic sight, psychic hearing, and psychic touch, but you can also use your psychic powers to bring about internal and external change. You can heal! You can move objects without physical contact! You can project your consciousness outside your physical body and beyond your present physical location. You can communicate with other beings.

It sounds exciting, even exotic. It sounds magical and miraculous. It is all of that, but so is every moment of your life and all the experiences you have. Begin to accept your psychic powers as being just as normal as all the other skills you have. Most of those skills have been learned through practicing exercises—whether learning multiplication tables, learning to distinguish subtle colors and sounds, or dancing *en pointe* as a ballerina. Whatever you want to do is possible when you accept that it can be done and are willing to make some effort to develop the required skills. As your psychic powers become stronger and your psychic skills greater, all learning and development becomes easier.

The more you believe in your potential to do these things, even miraculous and magical things, the more you will be involving your psychic powers in their accomplishment. This becomes your road to success. Later in this book we will write more about the importance of belief to your development. As the preacher says: *You gotta believe!*

The application of your psychic powers becomes automatic, just as walking became so somewhere between the ages of one and two, and talking became so between the ages of one and three, and so on.

WHAT SUCCESS MEANS

Being successful becomes part of your life. You are mobilizing greater powers and developing skills that make your goals obtainable. Know your goals; learn the necessary steps and skills to reach those goals.

Exercise, practice, believe, ask and it will be yours

Your strategies for success are actually to live fully. Don't compartmentalize your life but give everything you do the same respect and do so with enthusiasm. Enjoy! Greet every day with joy and enthusiasm. Don't complain because to do so robs you of your joy and sets you up for disappointment and even defeat. Don't feel sorry for yourself because doing so will give you reasons to be sorry. Don't talk to yourself with negative comments, complaints, and sour views because when you do you are creating those same circumstances. Compliment others in your life for the good work they do. Be optimistic because in seeing the bright side, you are creating the conditions for success.

In your psychic world you are connected to people, and in the way you see them and relate to them, you create a reality between you. When you think another person is shoddy, or that the person hates you, or that they're out to get you, you are actually creating the circumstances for all those things. When you start with something as simple as "Have a good day," you are creating the circumstances for both of you to have a good day.

When you're smiling, the whole world smiles with you

Success begets success, even if you start with imagined success. Your imagination is one of the most powerful tools in the universe. Imagine yourself as successful and imagine everyone you connect to as successful, and you create the atmosphere that encourages and attracts success. Success is not something that you can hoard, but it is something that multiplies when it is shared.

Attitude: look for success, and success will find you. It may sound simplistic, and it is! You are mobilizing all your emotional, psychic, mental and spiritual resources through a positive attitude expressing joy and enthusiasm in all that you do and invoking success. You are growing as a person, extending your awareness, becoming more whole and enriching your life experiences. Remember your connections—how the toe bone is connected to the foot bone and the foot bone is connected to the heel bone, etc. and all those connections leading to hearing the Word of the Lord. Seeing the connections in everything is empowering, opening your consciousness to higher perceptions. Recognize these connections as two-way streets, so that what you transmit from your end works to change the other end. Transmit what you want to receive yourself because you are creating reality.

Some people will tell you that success depends on connections, and salespeople will tell you that it all has to do with relationships, and others will tell you that it all depends on who you know. What they are saying is that it all starts with you! You are the master of your own universe, you are where it all begins. Put your own house in order.

Smile! And take the first steps to making your own future success.

References

P. W. Martin, *Experiment in Depth* (New York: Pantheon, 1955).

CHAPTER FOUR

MIND, BODY, AND SPIRIT
Interactions and Applications—
The Revelations of Quantum Theory

WHERE IT BEGINS

The revelations of information and quantum theory have revolutionized our understanding of paranormal phenomena and the practical applications of parapsychology.

INFORMATION THEORY AND QUANTUM THEORY

In the Beginning was the Word. *What* is the power of the "Word"? How can you interpret this expression other than as information or instruction to start and guide a process? The complete quotation from the Christian Bible (John 1:1–4) is:

> In the beginning was the Word, and the Word was
> with God, and the Word was God.
> The same was in the beginning with God.
> All things were made by him; and without him was not
> any thing made that was made.
> In him was life; and the life was the light of men.

Thus, the "Word," *information or instruction,* was the beginning of "all things," of "life," and of "the light of men."

Think about this, for it is profound. The universe didn't start with things but with information. It means that the mind comes before the body despite all appearances. It means that everything we know has evolved from that initial program—a program that has kept on changing and filling the entire universe with the amazing diversity of life and form and energy that we see now.

It means that for everything there is first of all a program of instructions, a *matrix* that guides the formation of the body, a matrix that guides the formation of stars, planets, people, animals, plants, birds, reptiles, insects, germs, etc. *Grasp the matrix, and you have the thing.*

We started by saying, "In the beginning was information," information that started everything, that produces life, and that is the light of men. Three things: consciousness, the universe, and life. A trinity that then manifested all that we know. You find such trinities at the core of many religions, many creation myths, in the Kabbalah's Tree of Life, in the study of logic, and in much the way we experience life as the middle way—balancing opposites.

But, was the "Word" the real beginning? No, it was the beginning of manifestation. Before there was the Word, there was its *Source* that we call God. God is all there is. God is everywhere. God is timeless. God is universal. God is the Source. By whatever name, with whatever image, or without name or image, we still recognize that there is a source for what is: *The Creator behind creation that is the source of creation.*

THE FIELD OF POSSIBILITIES

Quantum theory establishes that at the beginning is a "field" from which energy/matter emerges as waves/particles. The field is all there is. The field is everywhere. The field is timeless. The field is universal. The field is the source. The field is the matrix in which all things happen and which holds all things together.

The field is the source of all possibilities and the source in which possibilities of energy/matter become probabilities that are the matrixes from which things, life, and individual consciousness emerge. The field is another way for us to understand God as Creator, God as love, and God as consciousness.

With the new perspective given us with the advent of the computer age—also described as *the Information Age*—we see the fundamental importance of the *program*, the *software that instructs the hardware.* For what purpose? That depends on the *intention* of the user. Software is a series of *instructions* that are *communicated* to the hardware with the *intention* of producing certain *results.*

Actually, it is a little more complex because the hardware is first loaded with the *operating system* which is the consciousnesses of the computer. Software programs are the sets of skills that enable the operating system and hardware to carry out the intentions of the user.

THE POWER OF OBSERVATION AND INTENTION

Quantum theory deals with energy/matter at the subatomic level where it is nothing but packets of possibility, and energy is convertible into matter and vice versa. Science has learned that even the act of observation turns possibility into reality. Recently that understanding has progressed to the realization—experimentally demonstrated—that it is *intention* that brings change in the world around us.

Another trinity is the primary subject of this chapter, body, mind, and spirit. We are more complex than this—we have many bodies, or levels: physical, etheric (energy), emotional, mental, spiritual, and even more, depending on the metaphysical perspective adopted. We have also to consider the further complexities of the personality, the subconscious, the collective unconscious, super consciousness, the soul, and other terms that sometimes duplicate and other times extend earlier terms.

We can always add complexity upon complexity when we try to understand any aspect of the human being and of the universe. It's the nature of the mind to analyze and separate what it perceives into minute parts and then to wonder how all the parts work together. Such analysis is important, but sometimes it almost seems to obscure as much as it reveals.

Quantum theory shows us that everything is connected through the underlying *field* and everything does work together. This togetherness extends beyond the single person to include family, community, nation, world, and then worlds and levels that are both visible and invisible to us.

Quantum theory demonstrates that you can separate that which was once joined together, place those parts on opposite sides of the globe, and what happens to the one *instantly* happens to the other. This has been demonstrated at the subatomic level where matter and energy and consciousness constantly exchange their state of being.

Yet, we are all ultimately made of these subatomic packets that relate together in eventually becoming cells, organs, bodies, and states of consciousness. And we, individuals made up of these interrelating parts, also relate with one another and with our environment across the globe, and with other entities that we may, as yet, know nothing about.

In some sense, we are both our individual selves and full partners with other selves in greater and greater collectives and communities in which we may assert our separate self and/or function in unity with any of these greater communities. We are like glasses of water taken from the ocean, sharing the identity of the whole while confined—for the moment—in the boundaries of the glass.

At a practical level, what does this really mean? We say we are all children of God or children of the Goddess, or one planetary family, etc., but then we go to war with others who say the same thing but where leaders interpret the Word differently. Even within local communities of people, we say one unifying thing and practice another divisive one. Even within the close bonds of a family, separation and divisiveness happens—but while separation is, in various ways, recognized as necessary and helpful to children growing up, divisiveness is not.

But, is war necessary? Is killing in the name of God true to the Word? In fact, how is it that we let others interpret the Word for us when that Word lives within each of us?

Our physical body is a unity, but a unity composed of many packets of energy and information related to one another and organized into organs and various parts and systems that are supposed to function together smoothly and healthfully, but sometimes they too are at war, resulting in diseases like arthritis, diabetes, and cancer, and then there comes a loss of energy that we collectively call "old age."

We have the same situation in the larger collective that includes our physical body, our mind, and what we generalize as our spirit. (It is to spirit that we generally assign the other invisible parts including our energy and psychic bodies.) We say we believe in the inter-relationship of mind and body, and think that includes anything of spirit, energy, and psychic nature.

Now, let's do some self-examination. What happens when you neglect or abuse parts of your physical self—you eat badly, you don't exercise, you overindulge in alcohol, you indulge in psycho-active substances with names that end in '*ine*'—like caffeine (from coffee), nicotine (from tobacco), cocaine (from cocoa), and others? What happens when you overexercise, when you don't sleep well, when you spend your waking hours in fantasy, when you neglect your education, when you deny your psychic self, and so on? *You get sick!* And if you persist in this self-abuse, you die.

When you don't think of yourself from the higher perspective of a whole person, respecting all that you really are in body, mind, and spirit, you don't function with all your faculties, and—worse—you don't develop the parts and bring all their strength and powers into the person you should be becoming.

And when you don't do your part, and others don't do theirs, is it any wonder that our world is in constant conflict and that whole populations are suffering with diseases, hunger, and abuse at the hands of sick, power-mad, and abusive leaders who claim that God tells them to murder those of other tribes, other nations, other religions, and who tell their followers to strap bombs onto women and innocent children to blow themselves and others up?

What does this have to do with developing your own psychic powers and skills?

Think back to the foundational beliefs of the major philosophies and religions. One of the key factors is that *each* human being was given *free will*. Human beings can determine their own destiny; they can make decisions to use their minds to make their bodies healthier, to educate and use their skills, to develop their powers. *The ultimate meaning of life is to grow, and each of us has to make that choice to live a life of meaning.*

COMMUNICATION AND RELATIONSHIP

Earlier, we established the concept of the many packets of information and energy that have to relate together in the formation of organs and systems to make a whole person. *How do the parts relate together?* They *communicate:* that's what relationship means. You have to make the decision to communicate with your various underdeveloped powers. You have to consciously and willfully make the decision to become a more complete and empowered person. That's what your free will ultimately means. The responsibility to grow and become more than you are now is yours. It's the meaning of life, but it's your choice to give meaning to your life.

Medicine, and particularly alternative medicine, places a lot of emphasis on the mind/body relationship. It's a two-way relationship: what happens with the body will affect the mind, but most of us have little experience with how the mind can lead the body, and the whole-person complex. That requires the exercise of will, and an awareness of the parts that make up the whole person. You must learn to observe what is going on, and then use your will power and intend to make changes. Merely focusing on muscles, your heart for example, can activate the body's matrix sufficiently to restore harmony. Using bio-feedback techniques can be even more effective. With intention, and sufficient energy, you can make changes that can heal the body—with more intention and more energy you can make changes that go beyond your personal world and reach the larger world of family and community, and even beyond.

Yes, you can reach out to become more than you are and you can reach out to help heal the world of sickness, hatred, war, and madness.

The mind, through will, can lead the body—but it is difficult to do because we have to recognize the limitations of the hardware that is our body. The strongest and most familiar example comes when you are very tired and the body tells you to sleep. There are chemical messengers reaching the brain that induce sleep. Sleep is ultimately necessary for the physical body. The mind/body relationship can't be denied, but it can be controlled. We can plan our schedules to incorporate sleep time; we can get a medical prescription to help keep us awake in an emergency situation; and we can actually train the body to sleep more efficiently to give us more awake time. There are people who have sufficiently awakened other areas of consciousness to carry on with out-of-body work while the physical body is asleep.

One of your authors knew one such man, an attorney for his grandfather. The man never slept in a bed, but sat in a chair and did inner plane work while his physical body rested. He said he helped victims of sudden transition accept their death and move on to their new life between lives.

There are many ways to assert the mind's primary role in this relationship, and this can be reflected in our roles in communities and nations. When you compare groups of people to a body, you can see how a group mind can assert intelligent guidance over the collective. Just as the mind can lead the body into more healthful activities, so can the group mind lead a community body into rational activity in place of war, in place of social failure, in place of plagues of disease.

Your personal world is small, but it is part of a universal field inclusive of all other personal worlds. And, depending on your will, energy, and determination, you can affect that larger world, especially if you can work with other people to reinforce your intention through ritual and intelligent mass action. A well-organized and disciplined group working together can undertake healings, including healing at a distance; it can dissuade an enemy attack; it can promote positive social action.

Think about it: if more of us actually accept the responsibility of *conscious living*, then, even without deliberate and specific action, we can bring about change on a community scale reflecting the common belief and coherence of the group.

How to assert the mind's authority over the body's misguided instincts and internal conflicts?

That's the challenge: we have to reach down into the subconscious mind to make changes, resolve conflicts, and enlist its innate powers in a new vision of wholeness.

WORKING WITH INTENTION
TO BRING ABOUT CHANGE

Among the mind's most powerful tools are hypnosis and self-hypnosis. In the same category, we can use meditation and guided meditation, prayer and group prayer, biofeedback and focused visualization of our desired results. All of these are intention techniques that quantum theory demonstrates will bring about change at the fundamental pre-atomic level where everything that is manifest has its beginning.

In the beginning was the Word. And we have learned that this means the primacy of information and instruction. We can use the analogy of the computer, and think of how it is that the software instructs the computer to produce intentional results. You can insert new fixes in old programming; you can get rid of viruses that interfere with your programming; you can build a wall of defense against hackers trying to influence your programming.

You can even install a new operating system! We will write more about that later.

You have the power and you have the will. You can use your mind to call forth your psychic powers, and train them as skills, and you can integrate those skills into your whole field of active consciousness so that you can readily move into any necessary alternate state of consciousness to access them.

Stop for a moment. "Alternate states of consciousness" may sound scary or challenging, but we do it all the time. We constantly shift consciousness, from sleeping to awakening, from dreaming to dreamless sleep, from focused concentration to extended awareness, from feeling to enjoying, from speaking to listening, etc. In meditation, in prayer, in asking questions and listening for answers, in silent appreciation of the sunrise, in joyful adoration of nature's beauty, in song, in dance—all of these represent shifts into alternate states of consciousness. These shifts do not require the use of psycho-active drugs, or mortification of the flesh, or endless drumming. A trained mind can access different states as easily as changing channels on a television set.

THE IMPORTANCE OF CONSCIOUS LIVING

Even unintentionally we bring about change.

You have immense power—that other 90 percent that you have not been using. You can develop and train your psychic powers and skills. The power is yours and the choices are yours. You can choose to grow and become more than you are today. You can choose to develop and activate all the powers of your body, your mind, and your spirit. You can choose to accept the responsibility for becoming greater and fulfilling the plan that started right at the beginning.

We ask you to choose and become a full partner with the family into which we are all born. We invite you to lead a life of meaning and purpose. We challenge you to expand your consciousness to include your psychic powers.

We ask you to become psychically empowered!

References

Lynn McTaggart, *The Field* (New York: Harper Collins, 2002).

CHAPTER FIVE

THE NATURE OF CONSCIOUSNESS

Discovering the Power Within

This is a very challenging chapter. Think about this question:

WHAT IS CONSCIOUSNESS?

The *Encarta Dictionary* replies that consciousness is "the state of being awake and aware of what is going on around you." And *Encarta Encyclopedia* adds "No simple, agreed-upon definition of consciousness exists."

You can read whole libraries of books on philosophy, psychology, yoga, occultism, mysticism, and still other subjects, and you will find thousands of other statements to which you will respond: *not this, not that*, and you will feel that you left empty-handed. Consciousness can be discussed, but not defined; consciousness can be explored, but still you won't be satisfied with a definition, and you will still say: *not this, not that*. You can practice various spiritual technologies, and still not find a real answer to the question.

Until now!

Until now, about the best you could do is to relate the question to awareness. The dictionary suggests that when we are awake, we are aware. *But is that always true?* A person with a brain injury might medically be considered awake, and yet appear to be unaware. Even without such a brain injury, we probably have encountered people who are awake but unaware of their immediate surroundings if they are mentally focused elsewhere.

And when we are not awake, are we really without any awareness? No. You probably have heard reports of, or have yourself experienced, some kind of awareness while asleep, and even when unconscious through anesthesia or surviving a near-death experience. People who have been declared dead and then brought back have reported seeing all the efforts, in convincing detail, of their resuscitation.

It does not appear that consciousness and awareness are the same thing at all. But, there is an important relationship which we will explore later in this chapter.

A famous Catholic philosopher said "I think, therefore I am." What he was saying was that the ability to think defines a person, but he was unable to define thinking itself. And he later declared that consciousness arose in the brain, and existed nowhere else. And that is the general belief of many scientists today.

IS CONSCIOUSNESS UNIVERSAL?

If we cannot define consciousness, can we determine what is not conscious? Is consciousness universal or is it limited to humans? Can we deny consciousness to animals, to fish, to reptiles, to plants, or even to amoeba? All living creatures show evidence of awareness. Can we deny consciousness to dead matter? But dead matter, too, responds to stimuli. We even talk about different kinds of consciousness—such as body consciousnesses in which we acknowledge that the physical body functions well, even if we are unconscious. And are not dreams some kind of consciousness? And then there are out-of-body experiences which refute the claim that consciousness is purely a physiological function of the brain.

Perhaps we can actually say that existence itself has consciousness. We can't prove that it does not. Consciousness is universal—even in so-called dead matter. In the Jewish Bible, God says to Moses, "I AM THAT I AM" (Exodus 3:14), hence consciousness is self-defined.

THE RELATIONSHIP BETWEEN
ENERGY AND CONSCIOUSNESS

In the previous chapter, we several times discussed quantum theory and the field from which all subatomic energy/matter emerges as the beginning point of reality. In this chapter we will go considerably further in relating this field to consciousness as a result of some of the most exciting scientific developments in the twenty-first century.

Lynne McTaggart, an award-winning spokesperson on science and spirituality, writing in *The Intention Experiment* (2007), says the term "Zero Point Field"…

… concerned the extraordinary quantum field generated by the endless passing back and forth of energy between all subatomic particles. The existence of the field implies that all matter in the universe is connected on the subatomic level through a constant dance of quantum energy exchange.

Other evidence demonstrated that, on the most basic level, each one of us is also a packet of pulsating energy constantly interacting with this vast energy sea.

The well-designed experiments conducted by these scientists suggested that consciousness is a substance outside the confines of our bodies—a highly ordered energy with the capacity to change physical matter. Directing thoughts at a target seemed capable of altering machines, cells, and, indeed, entire multicelled organisms like human beings. This mind-over-matter power even seemed to traverse time and space.

Consciousness is universal; the field is universal. The subatomic quanta of energy/matter waves/particles emerge in the field. Energy arises out of the field of consciousness, but energy also *energizes* consciousness.

McTaggart suggests that human thoughts and intentions are actually things that can change and transform our world. She writes: "A thought is not only a thing; a thought is a thing that influences other things."

Here we have scientific confirmation of what many spiritual teachings and metaphysical systems have been saying for millennia—that our individual consciousness participates in the universal consciousness both intentionally and even without deliberate awareness of our connection.

The implications of this are enormous, and the ethical factors involved go beyond those of religion simply because of the scientific confirmation. Simply stated, it means that your every thought has an effect beyond the confines of your body and individual consciousness. It doesn't matter whether you act upon the thought or whether you speak the thought, *thoughts matter.*

If you even daydream nasty thoughts about another person, you have some small negative impact on that person. Idle inner gossip such as: *He's such a loser; she's so fat and ugly; he's a real dumb ass; someone should get rid of all those people*, all hurt other people and even—because we are all connected together—*bounce back to you!* How much worse when you vocalize, even such familiar expressions at a baseball game as: *Kill the bastard! Shoot the umpire!* All these have some effect, and when multiplied together in a crowded stadium it becomes possible to understand how a mass of people will sometimes do terrible things. *Thought has power.*

But, you don't have to be located together in a crowd of others for this joining of thoughts to have multiplied power. Even joined together through television and radio, thoughts have power, and distance is no barrier to their effect. Thankfully, in such examples involving competing teams, the supporters largely cancel each other out. But in mass political rallies, such as were used with great effect in Nazi Germany, there is no equal counter force. Thoughts can be manipulated by leaders to cause great harm even in the guise of religious authority, hence the necessity of knowing that you too are part of the I AM, the consciousness that is in all of us.

It's not just thoughts about other people that are harmful. You can harm yourself with negative self-talk, such as: *I'm so tired; I'm too fat; I'm too old; I'm a failure; I'm afraid; I think I have cancer; my father had Parkinson's disease, so I probably do too,* and so on. You talk yourself into an early death!

Psychic power is not just something nice that happens only to good people. It happens to everyone all the time. But psychic skills have to be learned. Everyone has some degree of psychic sensitivity, but they often are not consciously aware of their own psychic impressions and what they may be doing to them. You need to comprehend more of your own consciousness, and that takes effort. It's like the old saying: "You need to know your own strength."

If you want to see peace in our time, then realize just how important it is to change our ways of thinking. Realize how important it is to practice meditation and prayer in which you think positive things. Accept the responsibility for your own thoughts and actions rather than believing you can just pass it on to government, the United Nations, agencies, the Church, etc. They are all you! You are they! The enemy is us! Each of us has to do what we want others to do.

All metaphysical and spiritual teachers have the same messages: *Wake up! Be aware! Clean up your act! Thoughts are deeds! What you do unto others you do unto yourself! You are your brother's (neighbor's, everyone's) keeper!* It requires self-awareness to become responsible for your own thoughts. It requires self-awareness to perceive the negative impact of other people's thoughts on your psychic and physical health and well-being. And with self-awareness comes your ability to counteract the impact of those negative thoughts with the constancy of your own positive self-image.

There is a very real connection between energy and consciousness, both at the mass level and in each individual. Most of us suffer depletion of energy, and as our available energy declines, the power of our consciousness declines. Mentally we become more susceptible to the influence of others. We more easily become victims of super sales-people, of politicians who gain energy from the crowds of supporters, of leaders whose purpose-driven lives draw upon energy resources to dominate your own depleted energy field.

You can, and need to, defend yourself. Every person is surrounded by an *aura* of psychic energy that can, through visualization, be shaped into a defense shield to repel such attacks *unless you invite them in*. Unfortunately, when you wish to buy a house or a new refrigerator, you may encounter a super salesperson whose energy pushes you to make a purchase beyond your means. When the political season comes, you encounter politicians whose message may resonate with your fears and dreams and overcome your rational thoughts. A church minister delivers a message that may likewise play on your fears and dreams in a manner that bypasses your common sense.

You don't want to isolate yourself from others, but you need to be aware of their motives and keep your personal integrity high, your aura strong and your psychic shield in place. If their message is good and is rational, you will recognize it and be able to determine its appropriateness to your needs. Remember, you were given free will for a reason—and that reason is to grow and gain wisdom so that you—as a co-creator—act with wisdom. The Creator doesn't say to do as others say, but to act in accordance with your own conscience.

Look at that word, "conscience." It comes from the Latin *conscientia*, "consciousness," or *conscire*, to "be conscious," and to "know thoroughly." It's not something external, and not something from outside. It's a commandment to act with thorough knowledge, understanding the implications of what you say and do.

We are joined together in universal consciousness, but we also have individual consciousness and personal free will, with the single purpose that we grow in our own consciousness and wisdom to act with awareness and responsibility for the good of all as found in our connection to the universal consciousness.

How do we grow in our own consciousness and wisdom, connecting to the universal consciousness?

We have to become whole beings, bringing all our powers into unity, and learn to act in coherence and harmony with the fundamental instructions contained within the universal consciousness. As an individual, we have to become as wise as the universal in order to fulfill the purpose expressed Biblically: "God created man *in his own image, in the image of God created he him*; male and female created he them" (Gen. 1:26–27).

All the great religions and myths say essentially this same thing. All metaphysical teachings say that our purpose is to grow and become more than we are, to become more God-like and God-filled, not by following other people, but by learning and fulfilling the fundamental instructions that are the source of all being.

How do we increase our personal energy, to energize our personal consciousness?

The physical body derives most of its energy from food, but some of its energy comes from direct absorption of solar and psychic energy through the light and air we breathe. There are names for this energy: *the Force, Prana, Chi, the Life-force, the Tao, élan vital, God-force, Essence, Odic Force, Orgone, the Power, Spirit,* and others.

While we get this force through air and light, we can also get it through the arousal of *Kundalini* in the psychic body, and we can get it from attunement to the field, the universal force.

The simplest, but not the easiest, is attunement to the universal force.

The various exercises and disciplines of yoga, martial arts, Kabbalah, and shamanic practices are effective ways to increase the psychic force. There are other more complex disciplines as well, but all of these mostly involve breath control, visualization, posture and movement, and meditation. Chanting, meditation on yantras and other sacred images, devotional prayers, and certain sexual practices also connect to the force.

But the simplest is meditation and identification with the universal force itself. To become one with the source, while remaining an individual, is both the simplest and the most difficult. Everything in ordinary life makes it difficult. Life is demanding, and the meaning of life is found through fulfilling life while also moving beyond its attractions, becoming at one with the force without loss of self, letting the force flow through you in response to your will.

That accomplishment is the work of a lifetime, and more often many lifetimes. But the starting point is in your hands right now, and that is what we want to teach you in this book.

AWARENESS WITHIN CONSCIOUSNESS

In one sense, you are nothing but consciousness, an individuation of the universal consciousness. Likewise you are an individuation of the universal force. Mostly you are asleep. *The god within sleeps.* Like subatomic particles, you are mostly potential, and until you become fully aware of yourself, you are not fully real.

Your job, *if you accept this assignment,* is to become fully awake, fully aware, to be self-realized as a true agent and expression of the force within. That is the goal for each and every human being. Learn to *feel* yourself awake and aware in all you do, from the most mundane chore to the most sublime expression of love you can offer—whether to another person, to all people, to beauty, to knowledge, to life. Awareness is like filling in all the dots of your potential in order to become the God-man/Goddess-woman you are meant to be.

Become aware of the power within. Some locate it at the base of the spine, others the solar plexus. Some bring it into the body from the earth below and others from the sky above. It is really where you find it because it is everywhere and it is in you. The following exercise is experimental and not part of the program for developing your psychic skills that will be presented later in this book. It may help you prepare for new understanding of the interplay between your individual consciousness and that of the universal field. Don't feel disappointed if your results seem not to be dramatic, but continued use of this exercise may be very helpful with progressive results.

> *Close your eyes, and feel yourself sinking deep within. Relax as you breathe easily in and out, in and out. Look for a source of Light within. See it and go there. It may be that you will only feel it at first and only later see it. Feeling is as good as seeing. Find it and feel yourself bathe in it. The Light shines for you. It is the force. It is the God-force that gives life to you. It is the God-force that breathes with you that you may live. It is the God-force that gives you consciousness and the power of self-consciousness. It is the Light of men. Slowly return and bring the Light with you.*

Know and feel that the Light is always with you and is able to answer your every question.

References

Encarta Encyclopedia.

Lynne McTaggart, *The Intention Experiment* (New York: Free Press, 2007).

Joe H. Slate, *Aura Energy for Health, Healing & Balance* (Woodbury, MN: Llewellyn Publications, 1999).

Joe H. Slate, *Psychic Vampires* (Woodbury, MN: Llewellyn Publications, 2002).

CHAPTER SIX

SELF-HYPNOSIS: INNER QUEST FOR KNOWLEDGE AND POWER

Self-hypnosis is for Everyone

REAL EMPOWERMENT

Self-hypnosis can be defined as a self-induced state of altered consciousness that gives direct access to the vast reserve of resources and undeveloped potential existing in everyone. It's an approach, or program, based on the premise that you alone are your best personal hypnotist and growth specialist. Even hypnosis by the expert professional pales when compared with what can be accomplished through self-hypnosis. Fortunately, self-hypnosis, like psychic empowerment, is for everyone. It's a skill you can master for yourself, and once mastered, it's available to you on demand. The empowering limits of this skill, if they exist at all, are unknown.

Admittedly, we do not know all there is to know about the vast inner region typically called the subconscious. We do know, however, that through self-hypnosis you can tap into its resources and unleash a totally new surge of powerful energy. You can remove subconscious barriers that thwart your growth and impede your progress. You can retrieve buried but relevant memories, including those of past-life origin. You can uncover and successfully resolve traumatic experiences, threatening impulses, and deep-seated conflicts existing beyond your conscious awareness.

NEW GOALS AND PERSONAL ACHIEVEMENT

Once you've mastered the techniques of self-hypnosis, you can use them as tools for a nearly unlimited range of goals: achieving career satisfaction and success, increasing your creative powers, unleashing your psychic potentials, and promoting both mental and physical health. You can use self-hypnosis for such highly specific goals as losing weight, slowing aging, stopping smoking, accelerating learning, managing pain, and extinguishing phobias.

Beyond these, there's strong evidence that self-hypnosis can spontaneously produce, in an instant, totally new skills and knowledge, a phenomenon called *hypnoproduction*. Examples include instantaneous command of a new language and sudden mastery of an artistic or scientific skill, each of which could be explained as the retrieval of skills acquired in a past life. That explanation aside, it's possible that self-hypnosis could bring together a host of subconscious processes in ways that generate totally new resources and growth possibilities, a phenomenon we call *hypnogenerativity*.

Whatever our explanations of these amazing phenomena, it seems clear that successful self-hypnosis, in freeing hidden potentials, enriches our capacity for growth and personal achievement. Just as success begets success, the release of potential generates even greater potential. Consequently, human potential, when tapped into through self-hypnosis or any other means, becomes an unlimited fountainhead for new growth and self-empowerment.

SELF-HYPNOSIS AND SELF-EMPOWERMENT

Self-hypnosis is a goal-oriented approach to self-empowerment. We know that simply formulating a personal goal and stating it in positive terms is critical to successful goal attainment. Self-hypnosis goes a step further—it offers a workable program and flexible blueprint for your complete success. It's an inner quest that focuses on your stated goal and unleashes the resources required to achieve it. Once those resources are activated, you're well on your way to complete success.

When you've identified and activated those resources, success becomes your destiny!

Self-hypnosis is not an exact science. Paradoxically, its inexactness adds to its effectiveness. Although numerous self-hypnosis programs have been developed, no single preferred approach has yet been forthcoming. Induction, as well as deepening and application techniques, differ in both complexity and relevance. A person who is unresponsive to one approach can be highly responsive to another. Furthermore, an approach that is appropriate for one goal may not be appropriate for another.

For some applications, the most effective program is a combination of components drawn from several programs. That approach, typically called *eclectic*, takes the most effective, applicable aspects of other approaches and organizes them into a program that best fits your personal preferences and needs. It's an innovative approach that requires considerable exploration and practice, but you'll find the results are well worth your time and effort.

In the discussion that follows, we'll explore several programs for the induction and implementation of self-hypnosis. Although the programs are individually different, they are together based on a single premise: existing within are hidden resources that can be accessed and activated through self-hypnosis to enrich your life with abundance and power.

In your use of these programs, here are a few guidelines that will promote your success and help you to stay on course:

SELF-HYPNOSIS GUIDELINES

- Specify your goals and state them in clear, positive terms. *I will succeed* is far more powerful than *I can succeed*. Typically, the best results are obtained when each self-hypnosis session is limited to no more than one clearly stated goal.

- Set aside sufficient time in a quiet, comfortable setting free of distractions. The typical self-hypnosis session will range from thirty to sixty minutes, depending on the nature of the strategy and its application. With practice, the time required for inducing the trance state typically decreases.

- Dress in comfortable clothing.

- Do not practice self-hypnosis while driving, operating machinery, or engaging in other activities that require vigilance or concentration.

- In practicing self-hypnosis, give yourself permission at the beginning of the session to enter the trance state and to exit it at will. Stay relaxed, and don't rush the session. Affirm that your experiences throughout the session will be positive and productive.

- Self-hypnotic suggestions and affirmations are typically presented mentally rather than verbally.

- In referring to yourself throughout the trance state, use "I" instead of "You."

- Keep in mind that you and you alone are in charge for the duration of the trance experience. Formulate positive suggestions and affirmations that activate your subconscious powers while in the trance.

- As needed, use post-hypnotic suggestions and affirmations that will remain in force following the experience.

- Upon coming out of hypnosis, take a few moments to reflect on the experience and its empowering relevance.

- Be flexible. Try different approaches to find the ones that work best for you. The *eclectic approach* of selecting the best parts of several approaches and organizing them into a program that appeals to you personally can have a powerful synergistic effect.

- *Practice, practice, practice.* In mastering self-hypnosis skills, there is no substitute for practice.

SELF-HYPNOSIS PROGRAMS
The Handclasp of Power Program

The simple gesture of clasping your hands together can symbolize not only your capacity for success but your determination to succeed as well. It's a gesture that tends to build self-confidence, reduce stress, and increase motivation. Studies of the human aura have shown that this simple gesture tends to expand the aura and clear it of discoloration (Slate, 1999). When used with purpose, it can generate a state of balance and attunement while mustering the energy related to almost any task at hand. When applied to self-hypnosis, the handclasp can become an even more powerful gesture with wide-ranging possibilities.

The Handclasp of Power is a self-hypnosis program that uses the handclasp as an induction technique as well as a post-hypnotic cue. Although the Handclasp of Power can be used for almost any personal empowerment goal, it's especially effective for goals related to psychic development. Here's the program:

Step 1. Goal Statement. In a comfortable, relaxing setting, free of distraction, settle back into either a seated or reclining position and with your hands resting comfortably in your lap if seated or at your sides if reclining, state your goal in positive, powerful terms. Address yourself using "I" instead of "You" and affirm your resolve to enter hypnosis using the Handclasp of Power approach to achieve your stated goal. Remind yourself that you can at any moment exit the trance state by sheer intent alone.

Step 2. Induction. To initiate the trance state, bring your hands together to form a strong handclasp as you sense the inner attunement and balance accompanying this simple gesture. With palms pressed together, firmly hold the clasped position as the pressure builds between your hands. Note such sensations in your hands as tingling, pressure, and warmth. Continue to hold the clasped position as tiredness builds in your hands and expands into your wrists and arms. Take plenty of time for the tiredness to reach its peak and then slowly relax your hands as you count gradually backward from ten to one, during which time you interject suggestions to go deeper and deeper into hypnosis. Upon the count of one, let your hands return slowly to your lap or sides. Conclude this step by mentally affirming your success in reaching the trance state. Further affirm that you will remain receptive to each of your suggestions for the duration of the trance.

Step 3. Deepening the Trance State. While resting comfortably, you can deepen the trance as needed by such techniques as visualizing a tranquil, relaxing scene or again counting slowly backward, with each count accompanied by suggestions of going deeper. Another useful deepening method involves concentrating your full attention on either hand to induce through suggestion such sensations as tingling or numbness (either in a finger or the full hand) and then removing them, again through suggestion. This may require practice, but it can be a highly effective deepening technique.

Step 4. Handclasp Re-engagement. As you remain in the trance state, restate your goal and mentally affirm in your own words that all the inner resources you need to achieve it are now fully activated. Further affirm that you can use the simple handclasp gesture as a post-hypnotic cue at any time to activate in an instant the full empowering effects of this trance experience.

Step 5. Exit. To end the trance state, count slowly upward from one to five while suggesting alertness and well-being.

As noted, the handclasp of power is especially effective for goals related to psychic development. In controlled laboratory studies of extrasensory perception, significant improvements on a variety of tasks were noted among experimental subjects following self-hypnosis using this procedure.

Highly relevant psychic impressions will often surface spontaneously during this program, especially at Step 4 during handclasp re-engagement. An engineer, for instance, experienced during that step a vivid image of a collapsing garage where his vintage Corvette was stored. He promptly removed the car and within days, the building collapsed exactly as seen during the trance. In another instance, a psychologist who was leading a ground-breaking research study on the therapeutic effects of interacting with nature experienced during handclasp re-engagement the clear image of a beautiful woman he would later meet and marry.

As a post-hypnotic cue, the handclasp can be used as a powerful gesture to increase self-confidence, generate a more positive outlook, instantly reduce stress, and improve performance on almost any task, to list but a few of the possibilities. College students who used the cue before and during testing typically reported noticeable improvements in their academic performance. In their opinions, the cue was especially effective in stimulating recall. Several students attributed a dramatic increase in grade-point average to the use of this simple cue.

The Body Lift Program

The Body Lift Program, appearing here for the first time in print, is a little-known but highly effective self-induction approach specifically designed to promote psychic self-empowerment. In the induction phase of this lab-tested program, the lowering of the upper body downward and then allowing it to rise to the upright, seated position symbolizes the rising of your inner psychic powers from a dormant, subconscious state to an energized state of conscious awareness and readiness. In that fully activated trance state, you can exercise your psychic faculties by focusing them on designated goals, a process that actually increases your psychic powers. While this program is specifically designed for psychic self-empowerment, it can be effective for a nearly unlimited range of personal goals. Here's the program:

Step 1. Goal Statement. Specify your goal in positive terms and affirm your intent to achieve it.

Step 2. Induction. While seated in a comfortable position with your legs uncrossed and your feet flat on the floor, place your hands on your thighs and give yourself permission to enter self-hypnosis. Begin that induction process by first taking in a few deep breaths, exhaling slowly, and then developing a slow, rhythmic breathing pattern. As you continue to breathe slowly and rhythmically, close your eyes and mentally scan your body from your head region downward. Identify areas of tension and let relaxation soak deeply into every joint, fiber, and tendon. As relaxation soaks deeper into your body, visualize a peaceful scene and focus your full attention on it—perhaps a snow-capped mountain, a tree in a meadow, or the ocean at sunset.

As you continue to focus on that peaceful scene, let your upper body bend gradually downward as you count slowly from five to one with accompanying suggestions of being relaxed and at peace within yourself and with the world. Once in the stooped position with your hands remaining on your thighs, allow your body to slowly rise to the upright seated position, again with suggestions of relaxation and peacefulness. Mentally affirm that once your body is in the upright position, you will be in the trance state. Upon reaching the upright position, you can deepen the trance state by again counting backward from five with accompanying suggestions of going deeper. Once you reach the desired trance level, mentally affirm that your subconscious resources are now fully available to you and is receptive to each of probes.

Step 3. Psychic Activation and Empowerment. As you remain in the trance sate, you can activate on demand the resources related to your stated goal. If your goal is psychic self-empowerment, you can use affirmations and suggestions to awaken your psychic powers and promote the actualization of them. You can exercise as needed your precognitive powers to reveal future relevant events. You can experience remote viewing of situations and conditions related to your present and future well-being. You can exercise your powers to experience higher dimensions of power and draw enlightenment, support, and energy from them. You can interact with spirit guides and growth facilitators, some of which have been known to manifest themselves spontaneously at this stage of the procedure. During the stage, relevant images of past-life experiences often surface effortlessly with profoundly enlightening and empowering effects.

Step 4. Post-Hypnotic Suggestion. Before exiting the trance state, you can use post-hypnotic suggestions to extend the empowering effects of self-hypnosis beyond the trance state and well into your future. You can designate a specific post-hypnotic cue, such as lifting a finger or toe to activate your psychic powers as needed to take command of situations and unexpected forces that could affect your life and impede your progress.

Step 5. Exit. To exit the trance state, simply count upward from one to five while suggesting alertness along the way. On the count of five, open your eyes and take a few moments to reflect on the experience.

The capacity of this procedure to activate psychic faculties was illustrated by a pre-law student who had applied for a law school scholarship at a leading university. In Step 4 of the procedure, he experienced a clear image of a letter signed in green ink by the dean of the prestigious school notifying him that his application for a scholarship had been accepted. Within days, he received the letter exactly as seen during hypnosis, *with the same signature signed in green ink.* He accepted the scholarship and is today a prominent attorney. In his opinion, the award of the scholarship was, at least in part, the result of his ability to influence the future through self-hypnosis. *Could a strong expectancy state generated during self-hypnosis actually bring about a future event?* Given the power of self-hypnosis to activate the limitless powers of the mind, *why not?*

Aside from its capacity to probe and possibly influence the future, this program can have important therapeutic value. That capacity was illustrated by the manager of a building supply firm whose exaggerated fear of tornados seriously limited his life and interrupted his career. He typically slept in a basement bedroom where he felt safer. He obsessively kept in his possession a running record of tornados, and when traveling, he carefully avoided destinations with a history of them. He frequently missed important conferences or scheduled meetings because of inclement weather or cloudy conditions which were extremely stressful for him.

During self-hypnosis using this program, he experienced a vivid but fleeting image of what he believed to be a past-life event in which he was lifted from the ground and transported some distance by a tornado. The experience, though brief, instantly extinguished his fear of tornados along with all symptoms associated with it, a clear manifestation of the therapeutic if not miraculous power of past-life enlightenment. In his words, *"Self-hypnosis gave me a new life free from fear.*" Aside from the fact that the best hypnotist exists within yourself, we could further conclude that the best therapist, healer, and possibly miracle worker likewise exists within yourself. Equally as important, they are always receptive to your probes.

Although designed for use in self-hypnosis, the Body Lift Program can be easily adapted for use by trained hypnotists to induce the trance state in others, including groups. That application was illustrated by your co-author, Dr. Joe Slate, who developed the program and used it to induce the trance state in a group of thirty-two students enrolled in his course titled "Investigating Altered States." At the end of the trance state, the students were instructed to record their experiences and then share them with the group. Incredibly, two students seated at opposite sides of the room recorded identical experiences. During the trance state, they both viewed the full universe from overhead, but rather than viewing one universe, they each viewed two, one of which was the exact reverse of the other. Not surprisingly, their reported experiences led to a lively class discussion: do multiple universes exist, including parallel, or could such experiences be best explained as telepathic transference of thoughts and images, or as the skeptic might claim, simply happenstance? As previously noted, we do not know all there is to know about self-hypnosis, nor do we know all there is to know about ourselves and the universe(s) at large.

In a later class session, Dr. Slate used the revised strategy to activate the group's ability to mentally influence distant objects or conditions, a phenomenon known as psychokinesis (PK). During hypnosis, the group was given the suggestion by the professor that upon coming out of the trance, they would be successful in using their PK powers on demand to influence objects from a distance. Immediately upon exiting the trance, the group was instructed to mentally move a small Styrofoam model of a mountain across a front classroom desk upon which it had been placed and cause it to fall from the desk into a tray of water situated at the base of the desk. The energized group required only minutes to accomplish the task. Dr. Slate was quick to commend the group for having "cast a mountain into the sea"!

Given these examples, we can only speculate on the limits of this program and its capacity to unleash the hidden powers of the mind.

The Upward Palm/Past-Life Retrieval Screen

The Upward Palm/Past-Life Retrieval Screen is a self-hypnosis program specifically designed to uncover past-life experiences that hold special relevance to our personal evolvement in this lifetime. Rather than a complicated past-life regression approach designed to access large bodies of past-life experiences, this program is designed to retrieve small but important segments related to present-life adjustment and goal-related strivings. Easily implemented, it's a highly practical program with many valuable applications.

The three E's—Enlightenment, Enrichment, and Empowerment—are the major goals of this approach. The program accepts the concept that our personal experiences, including those of past-life origin, are never lost, for they are forever a part of our existence as evolving soul beings (Slate, 2005). They can inspire and motivate us while adding a new dimension of awareness and meaning to our lives. Their purposes can range from enlightenment to resolution.

Awareness of an unfinished past-life striving, for instance, can inspire us to move forward with greater purpose toward its fulfillment in this lifetime. Awareness of past-life trauma or tragedy can facilitate productive and sometimes instant resolution. Residual baggage associated with unfilled past-life struggles can be transformed into powerful growth resources. Awareness of past-life suffering can empower us with compassion for others who suffer. Even a past lifetime as an oppressive tyrant and the karmic baggage associated with it can become a powerful motivator toward contributing to the greater good and promoting justice in the world today.

The Upward Palm Program is a permissive approach that does not probe or invade the subconscious, but invites it from close up to share its resources. *It recognizes the subconscious as not only a content domain but a dynamic constellation of processes and powers. It recognizes that the wealth of our subconscious resources is complementary to consciousness rather than counteractive. It's a powerful component of who we are and how we function.* Here's the program:

Step 1. Goal Statement. State your goal of retrieving past-life experiences that hold relevance to your present life. Your goal can be general, or it can specify a particular condition or situation.

Step 2. Energy Infusion. In a comfortable seated or reclining position, with your hands resting palm sides up, close your eyes and focus your full attention on your palms. Notice such sensations as warmth, coolness, and tingling. Visualize a higher dimension of glowing energy and a bright beam connecting your palms to it. Think of the beam of light as your connection to the cosmos with its limitless power. Let the glow of pure energy permeate your palms and from there, flow throughout your total body, attuning you mentally, physically, and spiritually to the universe. Let every muscle, joint, and tendon of your body, from your head to the tips of your toes, become fully infused and renewed with bright energy.

Step. 3. Induction. With your mind, body, and spirit fully attuned and balanced, you are now ready to initiate the trance state, first by affirming your intent to enter hypnosis and then by counting slowly backward from ten to one with suggestions of going deeper interspersed along the way. Here are a few examples of suggestions that set the stage for induction:

I am now ready to enter hypnosis.

As I count backward from ten to one, I will go deeper and deeper into the trance state.

On the count of one, I will be in deep hypnosis.

In that state I will become aware of relevant past-life experiences.

I will become empowered to use that awareness to achieve my personal goals and promote the quality of my life.

As I count backward from ten, I will go deeper and deeper into hypnosis.

Upon reaching the trance state, you can further deepen it as needed through suggestions of going deeper accompanied by imagery of deeply relaxing scenes that include motion, such as a wind-blown meadow or clouds drifting slowly across a peaceful blue sky.

Step 4. Past-Life Retrieval Screen. You are now ready to retrieve relevant past-life experiences by visualizing a glowing screen and allowing images to spontaneously appear upon it. Take plenty of time for images to become clearly visible as if projected upon the screen.

Step 5. Post-Hypnotic Suggestion and Exit. As you prepare to end the trance state, mentally affirm that you will be successful in understanding the relevance of the experience and applying it to your life. To exit the trance state, simply count upward from one to five accompanied by suggestions of becoming alert and fully awake.

During Step 4 of this program, a physician who was an avid collector of pre-Columbian artifacts saw unfolding on the screen a wrought-iron gate to the driveway leading to a large Victorian mansion. A closer inspection of the gate revealed the letter W centered in its design. Only much later did he discover the significance of the experience. On a first-time visit to a distant Midwestern city to attend a conference, he experienced a powerful sense of déjà vu as he approached a certain street. He followed the familiar street until it led to a wrought-iron gate at the entrance to a Victorian mansion. The mansion and its gate, down to the encircled W, were exactly as seen on the retrieval screen during his past-life regression.

Intrigued by the experience, he looked into the history of the location at the town's local library and found that it had been the 1800s residence of a physician who was an avid collector of pre-Columbian artifacts.

Could careers and interest from past lifetimes persist to influence and possibly enrich our present lifetime? For this physician, the evidence was clear—his past-life experiences remained with him as a part of his evolvement as an endless soul being. Although he had at first questioned the relevance of the experience, his life, by his report, was enriched by the experience that expanded his understanding of his existence.

Global Search Program

The Global Search Program is a modification of the Upward Palm/ Past-Life Retrieval Screen. It replaces the retrieval screen with a satellite view of the earth as a way to obtain information regarding geographic locations of past lifetimes or specific areas in which significant past-life events occurred. Here's the program:

Step 1. Trance Induction. Use Steps 1 through 3 of the Upward Palm/Past-Life Retrieval Screen to induce self-hypnosis.

Step 2. Satellite View. As you remain in the trance state, visualize the full earth from above as if seen via satellite. From your overhead view, scan the globe carefully as it rotates slowly, noting specifically its oceans, continents, and islands. Notice the regions, cities, or other specific locations that command your special attention, perhaps by standing out as highlighted areas.

Step 3. Selective Perception. Select a geographical area of interest and zoom in to view it close up, paying special attention to such features as the countryside, roads, buildings, and people. Notice specific clues, such as signs, names of buildings, and styles of clothing that could specifically identify the location and time period.

Step 4. Past-Life Interaction. Should you decide to do so, let yourself become a part of the location and its activities, possibly by entering buildings or interacting closeup with people.

Step 5. Exit. Use Step 5 of the Upward Palm/Past-life Retrieval strategy to exit hypnosis.

Your xo-author who led the development of this strategy used it to zoom in on a highlighted area of Egypt where he viewed himself as a Pharaoh. Seated at his side was a strikingly beautiful woman with blue eyes and blond hair. His follow-on search of the literature found to his surprise one obscure reference to a certain Pharaoh whose partner, a beautiful woman with blue eyes and blond hair, was always at his side. For the psychologist, the experience helped to explain his lifelong interest in ancient Egypt.

Peripheral Glow Procedure

The Peripheral Glow Procedure is based on the premise that the powers of the mind are limited only by our willingness to use them. It's an innovative approach designed to unleash an unlimited reserve of energy and power needed to achieve even your most difficult goals. Here's the program:

Step 1. Preliminaries. While resting comfortably in a seated position, state your goal and affirm your intent to achieve it. Take in a few deep breaths, exhaling slowly, as relaxation spreads throughout your body. As you continue to relax, give yourself permission to enter self-hypnosis and use the trance state to achieve your goal while enriching the quality of your life.

Step 2. Peripheral Glow. As you continue to breathe slowly and rhythmically, bring your hands together in the so-called "praying hands position" and hold them slightly upward in front of you at a distance that accommodates a comfortable gaze. Take a few moments to gaze directly at your hands, and then slowly expand your peripheral vision to take in the full surroundings, above, below, and to the sides of your hands. With your peripheral vision expanded to its limits, let your eyes fall slightly out of focus and you will notice a glow enveloping first your hands and then the full room. Notice relaxation deepening throughout your body as you continue to view the glow.

After a few moments of peripheral viewing, close your eyes and relax your hands. With your hands resting in your lap or at your sides, you are now ready to enter hypnosis by slowly counting backward from ten with interspersed suggestions of going deeper and deeper. Upon the count of one, mentally affirm your success in reaching the trance state.

Step 3. Application. State again your goal and visualize your successful achievement of it. If your goal is business success, visualize yourself in the business setting of your choice with all the trappings of success as you mentally affirm, "I am at my peak of career success." If your goal is to lose weight, visualize yourself weighing the exact amount and mentally affirm, "This is the true me." If your goal is to quit smoking, visualize yourself being offered a cigarette and saying simply, "I am a non-smoker."

If your goal is the actualization of your psychic powers, visualize yourself enveloped in a bright energy field extending as far as the eye can see, as you mentally affirm, "I am psychically empowered—nothing is beyond my limits." More specifically, if your goal is to maximize your precognitive powers, let yourself visualize the future with relevant events highlighted, and mentally affirm, "The future is mine. I am empowered with the insight required to take command of it."

If your goal is rejuvenation, visualize yourself at your youthful prime, full of health and vigor, as you mentally affirm, "I am empowered with youthful energy and vitality."

If your goal is to find the love of your life, specify your criteria and visualize the person with those characteristics as you mentally affirm, "Love is my destiny." The possibilities at this stage are limited only by your imagination and your willingness to use the powers within yourself.

Step 4. Conclusion. Conclude the procedure by mentally affirming your intent to exit hypnosis by slowly counting from one to five. Upon exiting the trance on the count of five, affirm: "I am now fully empowered. Greatness is my destiny."

Aura Self-Viewing Technique

As an example of this program's further application, the glow appearing around your hands during the induction stage is thought to be a useful gateway for viewing the human aura. You can take that segment and easily adapt it for use, independent of the full program, as a method for viewing your personal aura. To use that strategy, called the Aura Self-Viewing Technique, hold either hand in a spread position at arm's reach and focus your full attention on it. Next, expand your peripheral vision to its limits and you will see around your hand a colorful glow. You can then focus your direct attention of the glow to note its color and other characteristics. The dominant color to the glow typically represents the dominant color of your full aura (Slate, 1999).

Rejuvenation Release

Rejuvenation Release is a program specifically designed for use at Step 3 (Application) of the Peripheral Glow Procedure. Developed in the university setting, Rejuvenation Release recognizes that aging, rather than being the product of a single variable—*time*—is the product of a complex interaction of variables, an interaction that is subject to your direct intervention. The program combines mental imagery, age regression, and post-hypnotic suggestion in ways designed to alter the aging process.

During age-regression to a stage of youthful prime, it uses imagery and suggestion to bathe the mind and body with rejuvenating energy, which is then deeply absorbed into the psychological and physiological systems to alter the aging mechanisms.

The program is concluded with appropriate post-hypnotic suggestions designed to strengthen the intervention process and to promote the continued release of youthful energy. Here is an example of rejuvenating suggestions recommended for use during the self-induced trance state:

> *As I remain comfortable and relaxed, time is slowing down.*
>
> *All my cares have vanished, and I am surrounded with peace and tranquility.*
>
> *Serenity envelops my mind and body as I now begin to drift into the past.*
>
> *Slowly, I am returning to the prime of my life.*
>
> *I can now envision myself at the peak of health and youthful vigor.*
>
> *As I view myself standing nude before a full-length mirror, I am enveloped in the resplendent glow of youth.*
>
> *As I slowly breathe in and out, I am absorbing the colorful, radiant energies of youth. A new surge of youth and vitality is now flowing throughout my body.*
>
> *As I now begin my return to the present, the wear and tear of stress and strain is giving way to the strength and radiance of health and youth.*

*Each day, I will successfully activate at will the power of reju-
venation throughout my body by mentally enveloping myself with
shimmering energy.*

The glow of youth in both the regressed state and the post-hypnotic
state can be of any color; however, pastel shades or the glow of white
are generally considered more effective.

This program is so powerful that, with practice, it can be used in
the absence of the trance state.

OTHER INDUCTION PROGRAMS

Following are a few examples of other programs which have shown
unusual effectiveness in inducing the trance state. Like the programs
previously discussed, each approach requires a comfortable setting
free of distractions. Once mastered, each program is appropriate for a
wide range of goals.

The Temple Touch Program

To induce the trance state using the Temple Touch Program, take in
a deep breath and exhale slowly as you focus your full attention on
your hands at rest on your thighs. Notice such specific sensations as
warmth in your palms, coolness on top of your hands, numbness, tingling, and even the texture of your clothing. Center your full attention
on one of your hands as it rests on your thigh, noting again its every
sensation.

Now let that hand become lighter and lighter, so light that it begins
to float upward to your temple. Tell yourself that once your fingers
touch your temple, you will enter the trance state, and that by slowly
allowing your hand to return to rest on your thigh, you will further
deepen the trance. Once your hand returns to your thigh, you can go
deeper into hypnosis by sheer intent or by simply counting backward
from five accompanied by suggestions of going deeper.

The Upward Gaze Program

To induce self-hypnosis using this approach, simply gaze upward at a fixed object, such as a shiny thumbtack on the ceiling, while resting comfortably until your eyes become tired, and then slowly closing your eyes as you affirm: "I am now in hypnosis. I can go deeper by simply counting slowly backward from five to one." This procedure is especially effective for such goals as reducing stress, increasing motivation, and building self-esteem.

The Sleep Arrest Program

Upon entering the hypnagogic state of sleep—that deeply drowsy, brief stage between sleep and wakefulness—arrest that state of heightened susceptibility by spreading the fingers of either hand and holding them in the spread position. Continue the finger spread as you present suggestions related to your goals. To enter restful sleep, simply relax your fingers and suggest, *"I am now entering peaceful, restful sleep."* This is an excellent technique, not only for achieving your personal goals, but for getting a good night's sleep as well.

EM/RC Procedure

EM/RC is a self-hypnosis procedure using certain controlled eye movements and reverse counting techniques. A research-based strategy, it is detailed in the book, *Beyond Reincarnation: Experience your Past Lives & Lives Between Lives* (Slate, 2005). It's a "how to," self-induction procedure designed specifically for use with the Past-Life Corridor, a program also detailed in the book and designed to explore your past life, including your preexistence, past lifetimes, and life between lifetimes.

The Finger Interlock: A Non-Trance Approach

Common to most self-hypnosis programs are three major components: *Goal statement, Visualization, and Affirmation.* By stating your goals clearly, you increase your motivation to achieve them; by visualizing them, you invest your energies in them; and by affirmation, you build a powerful expectancy that's essential to your success.

Fortunately, you can now take these three essentials a step further through a simple program called *The Finger Interlock*. Though not widely known, the Finger Interlock is among the most effective psychic empowerment approaches available. Based on the premise that complexity seeks simplicity, it's a simple gesture that activates in an instant our most complex faculties while connecting us to the highest sources of energy and power. It balances and attunes the mind, body, and spirit by using the hands as the physical body's antennae to the universe. It can revitalize your total being while enveloping your physical body with a protective shield of energy called the "Orb of Power." Here's the program:

Join the thumb and index finger of each hand to form two circles, and then bring your hands together to form interlocking circles. Relax your hands and affirm: *"I am now fully empowered."*

You can use the Finger Interlock almost anytime and anywhere, even with your hands behind your back. It's applicable to almost any personal empowerment goal. It can be used on the spot to extinguish or reduce pain, protect from energy vampires, enrich various mental functions, increase creativity, extinguish stage fright, accelerate learning, and dissolve growth blockages. As a colleague noted, "It could be used even when facing a firing squad!"

A college student enrolled in a creative writing course used it to generate ideas for a short story that received top ratings by her instructor and was later published in a major magazine. Another student, a graduating senior, used it during a highly competitive job screening interview before a hard-hitting search committee to activate a decidedly positive and productive interaction. She got the job!

Now equipped with self-hypnosis and related self-empowerment skills, you can chart your own course and determine your own destiny as never before. You can instantly add enrichment, happiness, and success to your life.

References

Joe H. Slate, *Aura Energy for Health, Healing & Balance* (Woodbury, MN: Llewellyn Publications, 1999).

Joe H. Slate, *Beyond Reincarnation: Experience Your Past Lives & Lives Between Lives* (Woodbury, MN: Llewellyn Publications, 2005).

CHAPTER SEVEN

THE POWER OF DREAMS
Doorway to the Unconscious

OPEN SESAME TO OTHER DIMENSIONS

Through the centuries, dreams have intrigued cultures from the most primitive to the most advanced. While the messages of our dreams are often concealed in a complex system of symbolism and disguise, there's almost universal acceptance of dreams as potential sources of enlightenment and power.

There's evidence that dreams have prompted important discoveries and scientific advances, influenced critical political decisions, inspired decisive cultural changes, and even shaped the course of history (Slate, 1991). Dreams can promote enlightenment and activate a host of inner resources, including our psychic faculties.

Given these potentials, rather than simply being peripheral influences, dreams become essential to our personal evolvement, as noted by Shakespeare:

We are such stuff
As dreams are made on, and our little life
Is rounded with a sleep!

Becoming psychically empowered depends largely on a clear understanding of the capacity of dreams to enrich our lives mentally, physically, and spiritually. As you explore the empowerment possibilities of dreams, here are a few basic principles related to sleep and dreaming to keep in mind:

WHAT WE KNOW ABOUT DREAMS

The typical six- to eight-hour period of uninterrupted sleep consists of four or five dream periods, with the duration of each period successively increasing from about ten minutes for the first period to approximately thirty minutes for the final period. As the duration of the dream period increases, the dream experience typically becomes more vivid, colorful, and easily recalled upon awakening.

Dreams commonly occur during rapid eye movement (REM) periods of sleep; however they have been known to occur during non–rapid eye movement (NREM) periods as well.

The frequency, intensity, and duration of dreams as well as the ability to recall them vary among individuals and for the same individual over time.

Although it's believed that everyone dreams, some individuals report never having recalled a dream. Fortunately programs are now available to promote recall of the dream experience.

Occasionally, the dreamer is aware of the dream at the time the dream occurs, a phenomenon known as the *lucid dream*. The lucid dream is often psychic in nature. It can awaken various extrasensory faculties and facilitate out-of-body travel. It can also be a gateway to the spiritual realm. Interactions with guides, growth facilitators, and the departed often occur during this dream state.

Hypnagogic sleep, that brief stage between wakefulness and sleep, is typically characterized by dreamlike images and sensations which may have little subconscious significance. Auto-suggestions presented during that stage, however, can dramatically influence dreaming and direct the dream experience toward specified objectives.

Hypnopompic sleep, which occurs briefly just before spontaneously awakening, is likewise characterized by dreamlike impressions that may have little subconscious significance. Auto-suggestions presented during this stage, however, can significantly influence your post-sleep state.

Although mental, physical, and spiritual factors can interact to influence your dreams, step-by-step empowerment programs are now available to intervene in the dream experience and direct its outcomes.

Recurrent dreams along with serial insight dreams hold especially significant relevance. Recurrent dreams represent repeated attempts of the dream to communicate important messages whereas the serial insight dream provides step-by-step solutions to problems or resolutions of conflicts.

The use of disguise in dreams, like dreaming itself, is universal, and some forms of disguise appear to have almost universal meaning. A towering mountain, for instance, typically represents personal aspirations or struggle for achievement or significance, and a large body of water usually symbolizes the unknown, including the subconscious.

Keeping a dream journal with entries made immediately upon awakening can promote both recall and understanding of the dream experience.

THE NATURE OF DREAMS

Dreams are often characterized by symbolism, metaphors, antithesis, or other disguises that function to protect sleep while challenging the dreamer to discover the dream's significance. Adding to the complexity of dreams and increasing the challenge to uncover their true meanings are the residual fragments of daily life, as well as past-life experiences that purposefully find their way into our dreams. Paradoxically, a complex dream message, once clearly understood, is seldom rejected, whereas direct messages are often dismissed. It seems we place greater value on dreams that challenge us to unravel their meanings.

Dreams are typically achievement or growth oriented, and as such they often suggest new approaches for accomplishing difficult tasks or solving pressing problems. Simply contemplating a problem briefly before falling asleep can result in the discovery of a quality solution. Similarly, briefly reviewing an incomplete task prior to sleep often leads to new insight and changed perspectives that can help you to complete it. Occasionally, dreams provide an important mental rehearsal for difficult or unpleasant tasks. The energizing effects of the goal-related dream experience can extend far into the future to bring forth important change and promote long-term success.

There's an abundance of evidence suggesting that dreams are often psychic in nature. Common examples are the precognitive dream that foresees a future event often in minute detail and the clairvoyant dream that views distant realities, again in great detail.

Unfortunately, the psychic significance of dreams often goes unrecognized and, in some instances, resisted by the dreamer. The precognitive dream, in particular, is often unrecognized until the predicted event occurs, and even then, the dream's relevance may be experienced only remotely as déjà vu. Unraveling symbolism and other disguises consequently become critical to our understanding the dream's message and effectively acting upon it.

PRECOGNITIVE DREAMS

The precognitive dream is particularly important in that it can generate awareness of a future event and, in some instances, empower us to cope more effectively with it. The president of a technology firm, for instance, experienced a series of lucid dreams in which a fissure in the front wall of the company's administrative building progressively worsened with each dream. Finally recognizing the dream as a symbolic manifestation of the company's financial plight, he took the necessary corrective actions that improved the company's performance and reversed its financial decline. The precognitive dream, once acted upon, actually saved the organization.

Even when the psychic dream's message is not consciously recognized, it can nevertheless have a powerful, positive influence. For instance, a clairvoyant dream, even when unrecognized as psychic, can expand our mental vision and increase our alertness of situations that need our attention. Similarly, the precognitive dream of impending tragedy can motivate us to exercise caution, even when we are consciously unaware of the dream's message. For challenging future events, psychic dreams can equip us with more effective coping mechanisms, even when we don't remember the dream. The power of dreams, however, is always increased by a clear memory of the dream and awareness of its relevance.

There is an emerging body of evidence suggesting that the sleep state is highly conducive to astral, or out-of-body, travel. In fact, one view holds that sleep itself is an astral projected state in which the astral body, the physical body's non-biological counterpart, hovers over the physical body for the duration of sleep. In that suspended position, the astral body is poised to travel as needed or directed to distant destinations while remaining connected to the physical body by the so-called "silver cord."

There are reports of sleep-induced astral travel during which distant conditions were not only viewed, but in some way influenced. In a rather unusual instance of that phenomenon called "out-of-body psychokinesis," an elementary school teacher reported visiting her classroom during sleep and arranging a series of books in a certain order on a table. The next day, she found the books arranged exactly as in her visit. In another instance, a university art instructor visited during sleep the storage room adjoining the studio where he taught. During the out-of-body visit, he accidentally spilled a container of yellow paint. The next day, he found the yellow paint spilled on the floor exactly as seen during his visit the night before. By their own reports, both teachers rehearsed before falling asleep the activities they planned for the following day.

While there are other explanations for these unusual phenomena, they do suggest the possibility of sleep-induced out-of-body travel during which distant conditions are not only viewed, but in some way influenced. Another view holds that such experiences are best explained as clairvoyant dreaming accompanied by psychokinesis (PK), the capacity of the mind to influence conditions or objects at a distance. Whatever our explanation of these phenomena, they clearly suggest the remarkable capacity of the sleep state to awaken our hidden powers and focus them toward specific goals.

DREAM INTERVENTION PROGRAMS

Only recently have advanced programs been developed, not only to promote awareness of dreams and their relevance, but also to activate the subconscious faculties underlying dreaming and direct them toward designated goals. In the following discussion, we'll explore three easily implemented but highly useful dream intervention programs. Through repeated practice, you can significantly increase the effectiveness of each program.

The Dream Partner Program

The Dream Partner Program is a multifaceted approach which uses pre-sleep suggestions to generate a powerful expectancy effect that directs the dream experience toward specific goals. It recognizes the dream as a positive, achievement-oriented process. It emphasizes the importance of working cooperatively with the dream as an active participant rather than simply a passive observer. The program begins immediately before sleep with the formulation of your goals in positive terms, followed by affirmations that during sleep your dreams will work with you as you work with them to achieve your stated goals. The dream, consequently, becomes your personal empowerment partner. Here's the program:

Step 1. Goal Statement. Before falling asleep, mentally state your goals and affirm your intent to work in partnership with your dreams to achieve them.

Step 2. Subconscious Resources. While resting comfortably on your back with your arms at your sides, lift one arm slightly and hold it in a raised position as sleep ensues. By continuing to hold your arm slightly upward, you can delay sleep, during which time you can engage the subconscious resources related to your stated goals.

Step 3. Visualize Your Goals in Color and Motion. As your arm remains in the slightly lifted position, mentally restate your goals and affirm that your dreams will work with you in your effort to achieve them. Visualize your goals using clear images with color and motion if possible. For instance, if your goal is happiness and success, visualize yourself enveloped in a bright sky-blue glow, the color associated with well being and success. If your goal is financial independence, visualize yourself enveloped in a golden glow, which is often associated with wealth. If your goal is health and fitness, visualize a shimmering glow of emerald green, a color typically associated with both mental and physical health as well as rejuvenation. Along a different line, if your goal is to find the ideal love partner, visualize that partner first at a distance and then joining you in an affectionate embrace. Take plenty of time to relish the experience.

At this step, your combination of images and motion has a three-fold effect: (1) it stimulates relevant dream mechanisms, (2) it's a source of pleasure that promotes restful sleep, and (3) it functions beyond sleep as a powerful force that promotes your success.

Step 4. Affirmation. As you slowly lower your arm to a resting position, delay the fall long enough to affirm mentally that you and your dreams will work together as partners in unleashing your subconscious powers and directing them toward the total fulfillment of your goals.

Step 5. Enlightenment. As you dream, engage the dream experience as a source of enlightenment and power while focusing on your designated goals. Let your dream become your link to the highest sources of power and enlightenment.

Step 6. Reflection. Upon awakening, reflect on the dream experience and its empowering effects.

Through the Dream Partner Program, the dream becomes a cooperative experience that initiates a powerful interaction with the inner resources related to your goals. Aside from that internal interaction, the dream can become your link to the highest sources of enlightenment and power, to include advanced spirit guides and growth specialists who are readily available to enrich your life and promote your growth.

That possibility was illustrated by an airline pilot whose wife had recently crossed over following a prolonged, painful illness. In his dream, he was accompanied by a familiar spirit guide to a distant, radiant plane where he joined his wife enveloped in a glow of blue, her favorite color. They embraced as she whispered affectionately, "All is well." That brief but profound confirmation of her peaceful existence in the afterlife was for the pilot an unforgettable moment of power. It required of him no further analysis or interpretation.

Along a different line, the Dream Partner Program is one of the most effective rejuvenation approaches known. For that application, visualize yourself in Step 3 enveloped in the shimmering glow of emerald green as you affirm, "Rejuvenating energy is now flowing throughout my body." Continue the visualization into Step 4 as your arm falls to the resting position. At that step, an interaction unfolds between your conscious and subconscious resources in which the rejuvenation powers of both are exponentially increased.

With your conscious and subconscious mechanisms united as collaborators, you become empowered not only to slow aging, but to arrest and even reverse its effects. Beyond that, your firm intent to alter the aging process tends to generate a powerful expectancy effect that can actually prolong your life. Through this strategy, you become the master of aging, not its victim. You become empowered to grow older in years, but without aging.

Energy Dream Work Program

Energy Dream Work is a unique energy intervention program that combines imagery, thinking, and feeling to generate a powerful energized state. It embraces the simple premise that dreams are thought energies in their purest forms. The program recognizes your capacity to initiate dream work and direct dream energy toward your stated goal. Here's the program:

Step 1. Goal Statement. Clearly formulate your goal and take a few moments before falling asleep to affirm your commitment to it. For this procedure, the most effective affirmation is brief, clear, and positive.

Step 2. Imagery-Emotion Linkage. As you become increasingly drowsy, form a clear mental picture of yourself succeeding in achieving your stated goal as you sense the emotions accompanying it. If your goal is to initiate a new project or to complete one that's already underway, visualize the end results of your efforts and sense your satisfaction at completing it. If your goal is to write a book, visualize yourself holding the finished book, perhaps noting its glossy cover, as you experience your feelings of accomplishment.

Think of your emotions as energies capable of turning images into reality. Affirm that your dreams will tap into the resources required to achieve your goal. Here's an example:

My inner powers will be liberated as I sleep. I will gain through my dreams the knowledge and power I need to succeed.

Step 3. Energy Dream Work. As drowsiness deepens, remind yourself again of your goals and allow related images to spontaneously unfold. Focus on the emerging images and think of them as the embodiment of energies related to your goal. As you drift into sleep, let your thought images unite with your dream images to become an energized force that empowers you to achieve even your most difficult goals. Allow the process to continue as you drift deeper and deeper into sleep.

Step 4. Post-Sleep Reflection. Upon awakening, take a few moments to recall your dreams as you sense their energies while affirming your power to use them to achieve your stated goal.

A gentle reminder: all your dream work will be enhanced when recorded in your journal.

Energy Dream Work is especially effective for goals related to personal enrichment and fulfillment, to include love needs. The procedure is based on the proposition that once you've identified your goal, you can increase your ability to achieve it by investing your energies and emotions in it. For instance, once you've formulated the essential characteristics of your ideal love partner, you can generate dream images in which you experience the pleasure of interacting with that partner.

The combination of partner imaging and interacting becomes a powerful force that can unleash your potential to use your dreams to shape a future reality. Because Energy Dream Work is a powerful strategy that can literally transform the dream experience, caution is recommended in establishing your criteria for the ideal love partner or any other personal goal.

Problem Solving. Aside from its personal development applications, Energy Dream Work has shown remarkable effectiveness as a problem-solving approach. Through this strategy, you can bring together the energies related to even the most complex problem situation. Once the energies are at your command, dream work embraces and organizes them in ways that result in quality solutions.

This procedure goes beyond conventional problem solving by introducing advanced concepts and highly creative applications. That possibility was illustrated by a scientist who was working with rocket propellants in an effort to develop an advanced extrusion process for loading large rocket casings with viscous propellant. Through Energy Dream Work, he worked in concert with his dream energies to design an innovative system that was both safe and effective. "Energy Dream Work took my knowledge of science to a totally new level," he acknowledged.

The Flowing With Program

The Flowing With Program is a highly permissive approach in which the dreamer "flows with" the dream experience, while remaining receptive to it as a source of enlightenment and power. Although the procedure is applicable to almost any personal goal, it can be used without stated goals other than the intent to experience the dream up close and to flow with it. This one-step program generates a positive expectancy effect by simply suggesting during the drowsy state prior to sleep that as your dreams unfold, you will flow with them to gain personal insight and relevant information regarding your present life situation.

The applications of this program can range from personal decision making to creative problem solving. A college undergraduate used the Flowing With Program to identify the graduate school she would later attend and to acquire a research assistantship that would fully fund her graduate studies. During the dream, she viewed the school from overhead and experienced a profound connection to it. She applied for admission and was awarded an assistantship that fully funded her studies.

In another instance, a contractor discovered through this program a dangerous fault in the design of a bridge under construction. With the dream fresh in his thinking, he examined the bridge's blueprints and found the fault exactly as depicted in his dream. Fortunately, the error in design was found early enough that corrections were readily made. Had the error not been discovered, the consequences could have been both costly and tragic.

A few years ago, a graduating senior in business administration used the Flowing With Program in his effort to resolve a difficult dilemma—that of choosing between two equally appealing job offers. In his dream, the two job offers, one from a financial institution and the other from a communications firm, were represented by symbols logically related to the organizations. He effortlessly flowed with the symbols to solve the conflict. Here's his account of the dream experience:

I am standing between two mountains. At a distance, I see an eagle and a carrier pigeon, both in flight. As they come closer, I continue to flow with my dream by reaching toward the approaching birds. The homing pigeon suddenly veers to my left and disappears in the distance, but the eagle approaches and comes to rest on my outstretched hand. I know immediately that we are friends.

The message of his dream was clear. The carrier pigeon, which transports messages, represented the communications firm—while the eagle, which appears on U.S. currency, represented the financial institution. The eagle resting peacefully on his hand provided the resolution he sought. He joined the financial firm, a choice that proved optimal. He is today a top executive in the global organization.

The Flowing With Program has been used by composers and artists alike to activate their creative potentials. A violinist who routinely uses this strategy experienced a dream in which he played a totally new composition as the sheet music appeared vividly before him. Upon awakening, he composed the music exactly as experienced in his dream. In another instance, an artist viewed a clear image of a painting that was to become, in his opinion, one of his best works.

The Flowing With Program can result in the *serial insight dream* which consists of a series of related dreams designed to solve a particular problem or generate therapeutic resolution. It's based on the premise that a gradual process can be more empowering than a sudden product, which can be overpowering. Flowing effortlessly with a series of related dreams can be profoundly effective in extinguishing fear, whether of past-life or present-life origin, by slowly desensitizing the dreamer to the feared object or situation.

That therapeutic role of sequential dreams was illustrated by an accountant whose persistent fear of water was systematically extinguished through a progression of related dreams. In the first dream, he viewed a body of water from a safe, comfortable distance. In the second dream, he viewed the same body of water from close up with people playing along the shoreline and swimming. In the final dream, he joined the group to experience the rewards of water-related activities. The series of progressive dreams slowly extinguished his fear of water and enriched his life. It provided further evidence that the best therapist, like the best psychic, exists within the self.

The Flowing With Program has been known to literally create new opportunities for growth and self-fulfillment. It can activate your psychic faculties and focus them in ways that enrich your life. It can awaken your precognitive and clairvoyant powers to expand your awareness of highly relevant present and future situations. It recognizes the concept that psychic knowledge, like all knowledge, is a powerful resource. *The greater your knowledge, the more empowered you become.* The Flowing With Program is among our best sources of knowledge not otherwise available to us.

DREAM ANALYSIS AND INTERPRETATION

A major goal of dreams is to advance our understanding of ourselves while promoting our growth and empowering us to achieve important goals. The effectiveness of our dreams, however, depends largely on our capacity to uncover their hidden messages which are expressed symbolically or indirectly through various dream mechanisms. Since no one knows you better than yourself, and because you alone experienced the dream, it logically follows that you are your best dream analyst. Successful self-analysis of dreams, however, depends largely on your awareness of dream mechanisms and how they work.

Although their meanings are often shrouded in a cloak of disguise, dreams are always purposeful and growth related, even when the dream's surface or manifest content appears mundane or insignificant. Seemingly unimportant dream material may be as critical as major elements that command special attention. A common everyday activity, a minor detail, or other seemingly trivial material can provide a critical clue to understanding your dream's underlying significance.

Even the day of the week in which the dream occurs can influence the dream's content. Analysis of dream journals shows that dreams occurring early in the week are typically achievement oriented and tend to relate to job concerns or long-range goals whereas dreams occurring later in the week or on weekends are more likely to be pleasure oriented and related to immediate goals and personal relationships. Perhaps not surprisingly, the more colorful, adventurous dreams are more likely to occur toward the week's end.

Dreams become increasingly complex when they include actions, objects, and settings that have symbolic significance. The dream of a distant sinking ship, for instance, includes action (sinking), object (ship), and setting (distant), with the action possibly symbolizing loss, the object symbolizing opportunity, and distance symbolizing time. A sinking ship at a great distance could, therefore, represent lost opportunity in the distant future, whereas a nearby ship setting out to sea could signify the beginning of an important phase of life, such as a new job or love relationship.

One of the most challenging disguises in dreams is antithesis, the use of direct opposites to convey the dream's true message. For instance, a dream of failure can represent success, while a dream of sadness can represent happiness. Antithesis in the dream's manifest or surface content is particularly common in the precognitive dream.

Fortunately, a close examination of the antithetical dream usually reveals a clue to the dream's true meaning, For instance, an attorney dreamed of a guilty verdict for his client, a female, who appeared as a male in the dream. The gender-reversal clue revealed antithetically the dream's true message: a not-guilty verdict which later proved accurate. In another instance, an engineer who reported a distressing dream of receiving a job termination notice from a fictional employer was informed a few days later by his real employer that he had been selected for promotion. The termination notice from the unknown company provided a significant reversal clue: a promotion by the known company.

As already noted, upon investing our energies in discovering the relevance of our dreams, we are far more likely to value the resultant insight and, when necessary, act upon it. Indeed, the subconscious self as teacher and the dream mechanisms as instructional methods compare very favorably with today's more advanced educational technology.

The meaning of specific dream symbols depends on a host of influencing factors; consequently any listing of dream symbols and their possible meanings is risky at best. The general meanings of certain symbols, nevertheless, do appear reasonably stable. The following list of symbols and their suggested meanings is offered as a guideline or illustration.

Dream Symbol	Meaning
abyss	emptiness, the unknown
action	life changes, progress, evolution
aircraft	aspiration, escape
animal	basic needs, prowess, dexterity
ball	femininity, completeness, balance
bat	masculinity, action, intent
bird	freedom, escape, vulnerability
boat	journey, opportunity, escape
book	knowledge, discovery, reserve
cave	unknown, hiding, unfamiliar
city	destination, social interaction, organization
climbing	striving, progress, determination
color	creativity, artistic interest
death	ending, unknown, loss

desert	unseen, emptiness, simplicity
door	opportunity, new beginning, past life
falling	frustration, insecurity
family	responsibility, obligation
fire	passion, infatuation, intensity
flower	pleasure, affection, afterlife
flying	out-of-body experience, freedom
fruit	reward, success, sensation
gem	new discovery, insight, wisdom
gift	good fortune, discovery, breakthrough
hiding	secretive, insecurity, uncertainty
holiday	flight, freedom, temporary
house	stability, safety, family
ice	loss of interest, survival
infant	escape, restitution, innocence
journey	change in career or relationship, new project
jungle	complex relationship, danger, entanglement
kiss	love, desire, longing
knife	aggression, anger, desperation
lake	inner self, the unknown, afterlife
money	status, independence, security needs
mountain	aspiration, challenge, achievement
ocean	universal consciousness, unlimited opportunities
party	social interests, unfulfilled needs, pleasure
playing	escape, gratification
racing	impatient, sexual strivings, competition
rock	determination, persistence, diligence
skiing	release, liberation
stairway	challenge, progress, success
statue	honor, ideals, reputation
storm	uncertainty, threat, emotional upheaval
sunrise	new beginning, opportunity
sunset	ending, transition
tall building	aspiration, hope

tombstone	past life, resignation
toy	carefree, escape
train	sexuality, journey, change
uniform	control, conformity
vase	sensitivity, artistic interest

By simply contemplating the dream upon awakening, you can often uncover the dream's latent content or hidden relevance. You can supplement that process as needed through an adaptation of free association that is used not only to identify the dream's significance but also to increase the dream's empowering effects. That strategy requires first reflecting on the dream and then focusing on a specific dream object while visualizing it and mentally calling it by name. Almost invariably, the symbolic significance of the object will then unfold, either in imagery or thought form. For instance, a stalled vehicle could represent a frustrating relationship that seems to be going nowhere. By further reflecting on the dream, your psychic faculties could provide relevant situational details and suggest effective solutions.

For complex situations, free association often focuses on a key object as well as what happens to it within the situational context. For instance, free association involving a dream of attempting to open a door only to have the doorknob disengage could indicate that your current approach in solving a particular problem isn't working. Further reflecting on the dream experience could reveal a more effective problem-solving strategy.

TAKING COMMAND

Through the concepts and strategies presented in this chapter, you can at last take command of your dreams and use them as never before to empower your life. You can work with them as they work with you to access and activate your highest potentials. You can use step-by-step strategies to unleash your psychic powers and promote development of your psychic potentials. You can use your dreams to solve complex problems, make better decisions, slow aging, break unwanted habits, improve memory, and increase creativity, to mention only a few of the possibilities. A deeper understanding of your dreams could significantly promote your personal growth and enrich the quality of your life.

Through practice, you can become your best dream analyst. You know yourself best, and your dreams are an expression of your innermost self. You can master your potential to uncover their hidden messages and apply them at will. Beyond that, your dreams can become a gateway to other dimensions. You can even travel to distant realities, access other planes, and interact with the highest sources of enlightenment and power.

Around one-third of your lifetime is spent in sleep. You can now take command of this important part of your life to promote your evolvement and achieve your highest goals.

References

Joe H. Slate, *Psychic Phenomena: New Principles, Techniques and Applications* (Jefferson, NC: McFarland & Co., 1988).

Joe H. Slate, *Self-Empowerment: Strategies for Success* (Bessemer, AL: Colonial Press, 1991).

CHAPTER EIGHT

SPIRITUAL COMMUNICATIONS
Interacting with Spirit Guides, Cosmic Growth Specialists, and Other Sources

WHY WE MUST DIE

What can we say of the great divide between the living and the dead?

We've been told that it is necessary. Why? Because of the limitations of the physical body, it must die, and the soul must go on to do other things just as a graduating student goes on to new studies or a new career. The physical body is a vehicle we have for a short time, but it is not us. It is beautiful, a source of wonder and pleasure, a means to life in the physical world that is necessary to the scheme of things.

But, the physical body wears out. We can replace worn parts, live longer through better nutrition and health practices, and we can practice systems of rejuvenation all to good advantage. But eventually, we die. At death, we move on and eventually return with a new body and a new personality and start a new adventure—all part of the Great Plan that is what we're all about.

We sorrow at the death of our loved ones and wish to communicate with them, to know that they do indeed go on, and sometimes we beg for continued interaction with them. But, we too have lives to finish and must go on to complete our tasks and learn our own new lessons. Life is a long continuum; physical incarnation is only part of the process that continues in other dimensions.

Still, we want to know that there is life after death, and to understand what the afterlife is all about. Those of us believing in reincarnation are curious about the life between lives, but most of all we yearn for an occasional contact just as we had before—like a telephone call from far away, a few words before bedtime or before the new day starts, the assuring touch that conveys love.

And, we ask for assurance that we survive physical death. What can assure us of that?

NEAR-DEATH EXPERIENCES AND AFTERLIFE SURVIVAL

In recent years, we've seen increasing interest in such phenomena as near-death experiences (NDEs), out-of-body travel, trance channeling, and reincarnation, all of which imply afterlife survival and the persistence of personal identity. The old view that personal awareness and being are logically and inextricably linked to biological existence has slowly given way to a holistic perspective that recognizes the spiritual nature of our being as endless souls. As a result, the study of spiritual communications with not only the discarnate but spirit guides, cosmic growth specialists, and other spirit entities has resulted in a holistic shift from formal causal empiricism to an eclectic perspective that recognizes multiple explanations, including the spiritual.

When we turn on the evening television we are greeted by many programs involving different kinds of interaction between the living and the dead. We see special documentaries about ghosts and haunting, we watch serials involving mediums who see and converse with the dead, and we meet program hosts who tell their audiences of communications on their behalf, bringing comforting messages from those who have passed beyond.

We read books with case histories of ghosts and haunting, of telephone messages from deceased, and of other communications that assure us that love still bridges the gap between worlds. Famous psychics tell their stories and we believe them because we want to. We feel that we need to have faith there is truly no death or life loses its meaning.

We need to communicate ourselves, or at least to know that it does happen.

WHY DO WE FEAR GHOSTS?

Why, then, do we fear ghosts? Why is a haunted house scary? Is it just fear of the unknown because there seems to be no interaction? Or, is it just that we heard too many scary stories before we became adults and learned to put away childish things?

Are ghosts and haunting proof of survival? Many think not and consider ghosts and haunting to be just paranormal phenomena and not earthbound souls. Still there are people who work to assist these spirits to move on and sometimes that does end the phenomena.

JUST A RECORDING?

Let's look at the other possibility that hauntings, usually associated with suicide, murder, and painful death, may be a kind of recording of the release of almost unimaginable emotional energy. Most haunting phenomena are associated with places with a lot of hardwood flooring and paneling, the kind of wood often used in making rich-sounding musical instruments. Hauntings usually are experienced at night when there are fewer activities and when people are often most sensitive to psychic energies.

We believe that emotional energy can be recorded just like sound on a tape recorder, and when a sensitive person picks up on that energy, it is often experienced as a vision of the dying person. Re-experiencing the event adds energy to the recording including the natural fears we have of the unknown. The recording takes on those fears and other people experience it with yet greater fear and horror.

But, what if it is nothing but a recording? Those recordings of energy, like other recordings, can be erased by overriding them with new energy, whether that of an exorcism or other ritual, or the joy expressed by new people, or even the playing of lively music. The feelings of fear, suffering, and horror experienced within a haunted premise can be infectious, and therefore, dangerous to sensitive people who would be wise to avoid the contact or protect themselves with standard methods of psychic self-defense.

One of your authors lived for years in a haunted house—actually with two apparent ghosts. One account involved a young servant girl who found herself pregnant and abandoned by her lover. Her family lived in another country. This all happened in the early years of the twentieth century when there was no counseling, no social services to help a lonely immigrant employed as a maid. She hanged herself in the stairwell leading to the third-floor servants' quarters. Long after the original owners sold the house, visitors would report feelings of fear and depression on those stairs, and sometimes a vision of a very frightened girl would be seen. With time, this ghost faded away as the stairs were used by young students of the art school that took over the old mansion.

The other story involved a young man who worked for the art school and gallery that had purchased the big mansion, and was discharged—incorrectly, it was learned—for theft. He was seen walking the halls at night, and once seemed to attack the person possibly responsible for his discharge. Your author, purchasing the house from the organization, always greeted "George" as a friend and soon George, too, faded away.

POLTERGEISTS

The poltergeist is another phenomenon not involving a spirit being. As the name in German suggests, it is often mischievous, causing minor accidents involving vases, clocks, and knicknacks. The poltergeist is not experienced often today, but in earlier years it was believed to be the manifestation of psychic energy projected from adolescents during puberty and reflecting their frustration and confusion with the hormonal drives they were told to repress and ignore.

Still, our greater interest in this book is not in phenomena but in real communication with our departed.

THE NATURE OF SPIRITUAL COMMUNICATION

The study of spiritual communications is based, first, on the premise that our existence as evolving souls is not limited to our biological existence in this present reality. There's an enormous body of evidence that our existence as souls is forever. The soul span, as we call it, is endless in two directions, both forward and backward, a concept commonly called the bi-directional endlessness of life. The soul is, in fact, from everlasting to everlasting. When we look forward, we see no end; when we look backward, we see no beginning. We existed forever before our first lifetime, and we will exist forever after our last lifetime. Within that endless soul span, we also existed between our past lifetimes.

Like existence, the evolvement of souls is endless. The purpose of our existence, whether past, present, or future, is to grow and learn while promoting the evolvement of others. Our spiritual communications and interactions with spirit guides and growth specialists as well as discarnate souls can facilitate that important process.

Spiritual communications and interactions are based on at least two major premises. The first recognizes that energy, although it may undergo change, is never lost. It follows that manifestations of that energy as survival phenomena could become an important source of enlightenment and knowledge not otherwise available to us.

The second major premise holds that multiple dimensions and planes exist, each of which is capable of interaction with our known reality. In that context, manifestations of discarnate survival, to include communications with spirit guides and departed loved ones as well as so-called hauntings, are explained as normal phenomena. They are often purposeful fulfillment of our need to communicate with them as well as their need to communicate with us. The growth benefits are thus mutual—they facilitate our evolvement while we facilitate theirs. Even our communications with spirit guides and helpers can be mutually rewarding. We've all experienced the satisfaction of helping others—it's the fulfillment of a basic human need commonly called nurturance.

Although numerous programs have been developed to initiate communication with the spirit realm, our most profound spiritual interactions are often spontaneous, including those related to nature. The natural world around us can, in fact, be among the most advanced channels for spiritual insight and power. After all, it's the spiritual dimension that underlies and sustains our physical existence, along with the universe at large. It should come then as no great surprise that comforting messages and healing energies are often conveyed through nature's quiet harbingers—a dazzling sunrise that inspires hope and signals a new beginning, a flock of geese in scripted flight that reflects the orderliness of the universe, and a flower that manifests the beauty of the spirit realm.

Even a lowly insect can be a messenger from beyond. That possibility was illustrated by a college student whose brother, also a student, had recently fallen to his death while mountain climbing. As she rested in the shade of a campus hackberry tree, a colorful dragonfly, its wings shimmering with an array of colors, lit upon her hand. She instantly felt the comforting presence of her brother who had recently completed a research study of the dragonfly. When the dragonfly finally took flight, she experienced, in her words, "complete assurance of his joyous survival on the other side."

In another instance, a still lake at sunset became nature's messenger of afterlife survival. Following the death of his young son after a long illness, a father, while walking along the shoreline of a lake they had often traveled together, saw for the first time a glowing orb lingering over the water. He instantly felt the comforting presence of his son. When the orb finally lifted, he felt along with it the lifting of his grief and the certainty of his son's survival beyond death.

Although phenomena like these are often attributed to coincidence or happenstance, they invariably offer for people who experience them clear evidence of life beyond death and spiritual communication between dimensions. As purposeful phenomena, they can meet a wide range of needs, both for those who cross over and for those left behind. Here are a few examples.

EXAMPLES OF SPIRIT COMMUNICATION

- A businessman, who died unexpectedly following a brief illness, appeared repeatedly after his sudden death in apparition form at the second-floor window of an old storage building behind his residence. The apparitions persisted until finally a family member investigated the site and discovered to his surprise a considerable sum of money stored in the building's attic. The businessman, having lost large sums of money resulting from bank failures during the Great Depression, did not trust banks.

• After a young engineer died in a plane crash, his wife noted on their first wedding anniversary following his death the unmistakable aroma of gardenias throughout her home. Gardenias, which were neither present in the house nor on the grounds, were the flowers she carried at their wedding.

• The apparition of a child who fell to her death from the second floor balcony of her parents' retail business appeared periodically on the balcony following her tragic death. The recurring image, always with the child smiling, was welcomed by her parents as a clear and comforting message of their daughter's joyous existence in afterlife.

• A student, soon after her fiancé's sudden death in a motorcycle accident, awakened in the night to see his glowing image at the foot of her bed. Smiling broadly, he reached forth lovingly with both hands before slowly fading into the night. For the student, his appearance was a clear message of not only his survival, but his unending love as well.

• Another student whose husband was a recent casualty of war often felt his hand in hers, especially when in familiar places where they had spent much time together. His touch brought comforting assurance of his continued devotion and hastened her resolution of grief.

Colorful glowing orbs are believed to often signify either a spirit presence or some other spiritual manifestation. On the campus of Athens State University is a magnificent Greek Revival mansion that now houses the college's administration. Over many years, a glowing green orb was seen at a window over the mansion's front balcony. A review of the building's history showed it had served as an infirmary during the 1918 typhoid epidemic. One account holds that a young man stricken with the disease ventured onto the balcony and fell to his death. As the story goes, shortly after his death the iridescent green orb appeared at the balcony's window.

As a part of their investigation of the interesting phenomenon, a group of parapsychology students met around a table in the room opening onto the balcony where the orb had reportedly appeared. Following a very brief discussion of the phenomenon, the bright orb nearly the size of a basketball appeared over the table. Since green is the color often associated with healing, a student in the group who had recently sustained a wrist injury reached forth and briefly placed her swollen wrist into the orb. By the session's end, the pain and swelling had left her wrist. After that, the orb became widely known for its healing energy. In particular, chronic-pain patients who visited the site consistently reported instant and in some instances long-term alleviation of pain. As a footnote, the student who had placed her injured wrist in the orb returned to campus upon completing her medical degree, hopeful of learning more about the orb and possibly, in her words, "bottling its healing energy." Unfortunately the orb had by then disappeared, possibly due to an extensive renovation of the building's interior.

Still, we often want more than these indirect communications.

SELF-HYPNOSIS AND THE AFTERLIFE

The mediumistic potential exists to some degree in everyone. Although it may vary from person to person, it is among the most empowering of all human potentials. Unfortunately, it is also among the most neglected and underdeveloped. Developing our mediumistic potential thus becomes a reasonable goal if we are to become truly empowered.

Once mastered, mediumistic skills can enrich our lives with new insight regarding the spiritual nature of our present existence and the afterlife as well. More specifically, they can be a source of comfort and strength during tragedy and loss. They can empower us to directly meet the challenges of unexpected situations and to solve our most difficult problems. They can dramatically expand our awareness and add a totally new dimension of meaning to our lives. At a very practical level, they can empower us to achieve even our most personal goals, from breaking unwanted habits to mastering complex mental and performance skills.

Fortunately, all the resources of the discarnate realm, including personal spirit guides and growth specialists, await our interactions and stand ready to assist us in developing our mediumistic potential and mastering the skills related to it.

In developing our mediumistic potential, it's important to keep in mind the spiritual nature of our existence as endless soul beings. Before this life, we each came from the spirit realm, and after this life, we will each return to it. We could call that return a reunion in which we take with us all the experiences of this lifetime. It's through developing our mediumistic potential that we renew our connection to the discarnate realm and promote our spiritual actualization. The familiar spirit guides we interact with in this lifetime could have very well been the same nurturing guides we interacted with before this lifetime.

Unfortunately, the negatives we see in this present life are all too often projected onto the afterlife. We are too quick to assume that, because this reality has its negative side, so does life beyond. The afterlife realm is a rich and nurturing place where our evolvement continues. To attribute negative or, at worst, evil characteristics to that dimension is to contradict the essential nature of the afterlife as a positive place for our continued growth and fulfillment. There's a mountain of evidence clearly indicating that our transition to the other side initiates an enriched continuation of our spiritual evolvement as endless souls.

THE PRESERVATION OF PEAK GROWTH

There's also abundant evidence that, at our transition, we regain the highest peak of our past development, a concept we call "the preservation of peak growth." Should our growth in a given lifetime have been unfortunately arrested, we could have reached that peak early in life, even in childhood. On the other hand, if our growth continued throughout a lifetime, our peak would be reached only at death, which can itself be a peak experience. Because our past-life experiences are never lost, we take them with us to the discarnate realm where they become, whatever their nature, important growth resources. Even the cruelest of despots at death will regain the past peak of his growth, which could have been in early childhood. He will, however, take to the other side the totality of his lifetime of experiences which he must resolve, either in the afterlife or in another lifetime.

In past-life regression, it isn't unusual to discover a past lifetime that was the antithesis of a present lifetime. A criminal in a past lifetime may be a caring humanitarian in the present lifetime. That's one way karma works—there are other ways, of course, including our work in the afterlife to right our wrongs. There is, incidentally, absolutely no evidence that generous humanitarians in a past lifetime became cruel despots in a later lifetime. There is, likewise, absolutely no evidence that a cruel despot remained a cruel despot in the afterlife. It is plausible, however, that even the most advanced spirit guides and growth specialists successfully transformed their own past misdeeds into positive growth resources and thus became empowered to help others do the same. The discarnate realm sets a standard of good toward which we all should strive, whether in this lifetime or the beyond.

With these concepts in mind, we can develop our mediumistic powers and exercise them with confidence that they will promote our growth while contributing to the growth of others, including in some instances helping souls on the other side. Our interactions with the departed can at once fulfill not only our needs to interact with them but their needs to interact with us as well.

Your mediumistic potential is a part of your basic makeup as a spirit being—it challenges you to activate and develop it to its fullest. Let nothing hold you back in meeting that important challenge.

Self-Hypnosis and Mediumistic Power

Clearly, developing your mediumistic potential is essential to your spiritual evolvement, and self-hypnosis is one of the most effective ways of achieving that important goal. Self-hypnosis can connect you to the spirit realm with its abundance of empowerment resources.

THE TEMPLE TOUCH: CONNECTING TO THE SPIRIT REALM

Although other induction programs are available, one of the best and yet simplest is the "temple touch." It's based on the premise that your best personal medium, like your best hypnotist, exists within yourself. The temple touch empowers you to get in touch with that medium and exercise its powers. Here's the program, which requires approximately one hour in a quiet setting free of distractions.

Step 1. Relaxation. Settle back into a comfortable upright or reclining position, and with your hands resting on your thighs, close your eyes and take in a few deep breaths, exhaling slowly. As you breathe slowly and rhythmically, progressively relax your body from your forehead downward to the very tips of your toes. Absorb the relaxation deeper and deeper into your body. As your body remains deeply relaxed, give yourself permission to enter hypnosis and affirm that you will be in full control throughout the trance experience. Further affirm that you can at any moment exit the trance state at will.

Step 2. Induction. Begin induction by slowly counting backward from ten, with suggestions of relaxation and drowsiness presented along the way. Upon the count of one, concentrate your full attention on your hands, noticing such sensations as warmth, heaviness, tingling, and so forth. Next, center your full attention on one hand and let that hand become lighter and lighter until it begins to rise slowly to your temple. Mentally affirm, again in your own words, that when your hand touches your temple, you will enter a trance state in which your mediumistic potentials will be fully activated. This gesture, called temple touch, initiates your interaction with the spirit realm. Let your hand, after touching your temple, return to rest in your lap.

Step 3. Spirit Interaction. With your hand resting in your lap, let impressions of spiritual relevance emerge, to include images of spirit guides and the departed. You can then interact and communicate with them to gain insight, guidance, and in some instances, resolution. Take as much time as you need for the interaction to run its course.

Step 4. Post-Hypnotic Suggestion. Before ending the trance state, you can give yourself the post-hypnotic suggestion that by simply touching your temple, you can activate at will your mediumistic abilities.

Step 5. Reflection. End the trance by slowly counting upward from one to five. Upon ending the trance, take plenty of time to reflect on the experience.

With repeated practice, you will find that entering the trance state using this program becomes easier and the results more productive. The trance and the interactions that accompany it can become peak experiences in which life-changing insight and powerful infusions of energy will emerge.

A psychologist specializing in the treatment of depression interacted in Step three of this program with a familiar spirit guide enveloped in iridescent green, the color often associated with healing. She, in fact, knew upon his appearance that the guide was a healing entity who had been with her over many years. Through her interactions with him, she discovered that she herself had struggled with depression in each of her two most recent lifetimes, one of which had ended in suicide. In the discarnate state prior to her present lifetime, she was at last able to overcome depression with the help of her spirit guide. As a psychologist, she now devotes her practice to helping others cope with depression. By her report, she often senses her guide's healing presence during therapy sessions with her patients, some of them with suicidal symptoms. Her guide, whom she calls Rex, has become, again by her report, a highly competent cotherapist. She uses the subtle temple touch to interact with him as needed. She's convinced that by developing her mediumistic powers, she has dramatically improved her effectiveness as a psychotherapist.

With practice and experience, you can master the temple touch as a post-hypnotic cue to activate your mediumistic powers in an instant. When working in mediumistic sessions with groups, this simple gesture can initiate highly productive interactions with discarnates, including those associated in some way with members of the group.

Although souls on the other side often wish simply to exchange greetings with a family member or friend left behind, they occasionally seek resolution of deeply personal concerns, which can range from unfinished projects to the welfare of a beloved animal companion they left behind. Perhaps not surprisingly, animals on the other side often interact with the caregivers they left behind, thus adding to a building body of evidence that animals not only exist in the afterlife, they too are mediumistic.

The temple touch is a mediumistic development program that requires considerable practice, but it is well worth your effort. Once you've mastered this program, it can enrich your life with abundant new growth opportunities available only in the spirit world. Through the temple touch, the discarnate realm becomes a present reality rather than a distant, inaccessible realm. You'll discover it's a dimension as close as the air you breathe.

HYPNAGOGIC ARREST

The hypnagogic state, that brief stage between wakefulness and sleep, can provide a valuable link to the spirit realm in which empowering interactions with discarnates and other spirit entities can unfold. Through this step-by step program called "Hypnagogic Arrest," you can arrest hypnagogic sleep and use it as a trance state to activate your mediumistic powers. In that state of arrested sleep, you can communicate with spiritual guides and growth specialists as well as departed loved ones and friends. Beyond these applications, you can use arrested sleep to generate the so-called mediumistic dream in which the later dream state takes on mediumistic functions.

The goal of hypnagogic arrest is thus twofold: first, to activate your mediumistic potential during the arrest state, and second, to promote mediumistic interactions during the sleep state that follows. Like the temple touch previously discussed, hypnagogic arrest is based on the simple premise that your best personal medium exists within yourself. Hypnagogic arrest empowers you to access and activate that potent source of enlightenment and power.

Step 1. Your Goal. While resting comfortably before falling asleep, briefly reflect on the spiritual nature of your being and the relevance of mediumistic interactions to your personal development. Mentally affirm your goal of activating your mediumistic abilities during sleep and using them to enrich your life. You may at this step wish to specify certain personal goals.

Step 2. Delay Sleep while Affirming Intent. Upon becoming drowsy, spread the fingers of either hand and retain the spread position to delay sleep. Again, mentally affirm your intent to interact with the spiritual dimension.

Step 3. Mediumistic Impressions. Continue to hold the finger-spread position and allow mediumistic images and impressions to unfold. At this point, you can focus on certain familiar spirit entities, such as personal guides or the departed, but without specifically calling them forth. Remain open to interactions while keeping in mind that forceful, directed interactions are typically nonproductive.

Step 4. Spirit Interaction. As you remain in a drowsy, receptive state, familiar spirit guides along with other spirit entities will almost always come forth. Among them could be departed loved ones, friends, and even beloved animals. Take plenty of time to interact with them while continuing to delay sleep by keeping your fingers in the spread position.

Step 5. Sleep Interactions. As drowsiness deepens, slowly relax your fingers and tell yourself that during sleep, you will continue the in-progress interactions while remaining receptive to others.

Step 6. Sleep. To induce sleep, let your fingers slowly relax.

Step 7. Reflection. Upon awakening, record your mediumistic pre-sleep and dream experiences and reflect on their empowering relevance.

As with most psychic empowerment programs, the effectiveness of hypnagogic arrest increases with practice. It can be used regularly for initiating interactions with unlimited empowerment possibilities. As a footnote, the simple finger-spread technique can be used independently of the full program to induce healthful sleep. It's an excellent way to get a good night's rest.

A defense attorney and her husband who regularly use this strategy together reported a recurring visitation of a familiar guide who always announced his presence by gently tapping three times on the headboard of their brass bed. Following the interaction, another three taps on the headboard signaled the guide's departure. According to the attorney, it was not unusual for the guide to bring forth new information related to cases in progress. In court sessions while arguing difficult cases, she often sensed the guide's supportive presence.

In another instance, a college senior majoring in biology used hypnagogic arrest in her search for a teaching position. The familiar spirit guide, who appeared first during the arrest state and then remained present during sleep, revealed a dream-like image of a certain high-school with a vacant laboratory. The student checked with the school the following day to discover it had a vacancy for a biology teacher. She promptly applied for the position and was immediately hired.

As noted, deceased family members often come forth, either during the arrest state or in later sleep. A college student experienced during hypnagogic arrest a deeply meaningful interaction with his recently deceased grandmother who had raised him. During the interaction, his grandmother greeted him with a unique, but familiar gesture—the joining of the thumb and index finger of each hand to form two circles. It was the gesture his grandmother always used when congratulating him for making good grades or winning at sports. In the interaction, his grandmother wore a flowing garment of light blue, her favorite color.

A gathering of entities will occasionally appear during the hypnagogic arrest state. In a rather unusual instance, a mother was visited during that state by her recently deceased child, accompanied by several other children. They were gleefully engaging in recreational activities in a garden-like setting. Watching over them was a gentle, guiding presence. The experience was for the mother a profound moment of comfort and peace. It was also a moment of insight: it changed her views of life, death, and the afterlife.

Although many spiritual communications seem to signify a natural coming together of dimensions, complex interactions that are not always easily understood do occur. Examples are the profound mystical experiences and those rare peak moments in life when we experience the highest sources of wisdom and power, both within ourselves and beyond.

INTERACTIONS WITH SPIRIT GUIDES AND GROWTH SPECIALISTS

As we have observed before, *growth* seems to be the all-encompassing meaning to life, no matter in what form or place it manifests. That necessarily suggests that we continue to grow and evolve after death and that there are souls both less and far more advanced than the average person.

Aside from our own growth, another characteristic of life as we know it is that of readily helping others. We reach out helping hands both literally and figuratively in many ways to many people, even as small financial contributions, or ready professional advice, or in healing prayers. It should come as no surprise that those more advanced souls do seek to help those less advanced where possible, and particularly when invited.

Sometimes the help of spirit guides and advanced growth specialists will be overt, but mostly it occurs as an intervention that is more like luck than something personal. One of your authors, as a young boy, was playing on a frozen stream about twenty feet away from the edge of a hundred-foot drop that made a beautiful falls in the summer. Suddenly he started sliding helplessly toward that drop-off with nothing to stop him—except, at the last minute, he did stop and crawled very carefully off the ice.

Intervention? We can't say, but nothing else can account for it.

But you can communicate with your spirit guide. You have to provide the means to do so by opening your imagination and letting an image build itself. Just, in essence, ask, "What does my guide look like," and let the image form. It may take several attempts, but do not impose any preconceptions about what you think your guide should look like. Just let it happen. At first, just enjoy the companionship. For example, you might see yourself sitting with your guide, enjoying the sunrise, and then thank him/her for sharing the moment together. Repeat this daily.

As the image becomes stronger and the relationship more firmly established, ask single questions or make simple requests. You should record your conversations in a journal. Ask about the nature of your psychic development, ask about the nature of your psychic world, ask about the health of the world, and so on. Don't make demands, don't ask difficult questions. Again, as the relationship strengthens, the question can become more specific and more practical, but don't push it too fast, and be careful that you are not projecting your own ideas and expectations onto this image—which is only a vehicle for your guide.

In times of need, you will feel the comforting presence of your guide. Remember that this is a psychic (or spiritual) and not a physical being. In general, expect help in the form of advice and answers to questions. Don't expect your guide to fix things for you. Don't expect your guide to return a straying lover to you. It may happen, but that's not the kind of intervention that can be requested. As the relationship develops further, you will understand better what you can ask of your guide and what you can expect.

Your guide or guides are not the only spiritual entities you can communicate with, but they are the most immediate. Don't be too rigid in defining these entities, which may include angels, familiars, family, friends, and teachers from previous lives. And they are not limited to the deceased but may include astral visitors who are still alive in their physical bodies.

COMMUNICATION WITH GODS, GODDESSES, AND HIGHER COSMIC POWERS

Your psychic world is rich in resources, but much depends on what you do to enable entities to work with you. One very dramatic and powerful example is drawn from the practice of magic. It is called the "assumption of god-forms." We are only mentioning this, as going into it requires considerable training and understanding. The reference list provides the necessary resources.

The assumption of a god-form is somewhat similar to the image building you've already learned in providing an imaginary (astral) vehicle for your guide. A god-form is specific and is assumed to tap into that god's specialized powers and resources. The "god" we are talking about is not God the universal creator, but those lesser gods for the Pagan religions, who rule particular functions like love, war, commerce, fertility, wealth, and so on. In your imagination you build the form for the god/goddess as found in mythical or religious sources, and then put it on like a garment to become an astral manifestation of that deity with its powers and wisdom. It is a technique like mediumship where the invoked deity replaces the personality temporarily.

To benefit requires careful preparation. You need to learn all you can about the particular god, then using self-hypnosis instruct yourself to ask of the deity specific questions related to his special function and remember the answers when you awake from the trance state. The real goal is to infuse yourself with the god's knowledge and attributes, and then go on to work with other gods as well.

Can you likewise work with yet higher cosmic powers?

CAN WE COMMUNICATE WITH GOD?

The answer is a tentative "yes," but the preparatory work is demanding and extensive. It's up to you to prepare the vehicles or houses for the deity in magnificent detail.

You can see that "psychic empowerment" is much more than becoming psychic! Empowerment involves growth and development of all that the human spirit is capable of, and that is infinite. Empowerment means to be all that you can be, more than you can even, as yet, imagine. Our goal is to become one with our source, the Creator, God. We are born of God, and we return to God—after a long journey and many lessons.

References

Melita Denning and Osborne Phillips, *Practical Guide to Psychic Self-Defense* (Woodbury, MN: Llewellyn Publications, 2001).

Frater U∴D∴ *High Magic II* (Woodbury, MN: Llewellyn, 2008).

CHAPTER NINE

HIGHER REALMS OF POWER
Cosmic Planes and Inner Dimensions

Man's mind mirrors a universe that mirrors man's mind.
—Joseph Chilton Pearce

The problem with trying to separate perception from reality
in the confidence crisis gripping global finance is that perception
is the biggest factor shaping reality, as a host of voices
from the financial front lines demonstrates.
—Joseph Schuman, Wall Street Journal Online,
September 18, 2008

THE REALITY OF REALITY

Man is made in God's image, and God is all—hence man is a miniature
of the universe, a microcosm of the macrocosm.

THE STRUCTURE OF THE INVISIBLE UNIVERSE

Everything we've written about the invisible parts of man is true
about the invisible parts of the universe. Just as there are levels of consciousness, so are there levels, or planes, of the universe. But, man and
universe all have the same point of origin in the universal field of subatomic energy/matter packets. As the universe burst into manifestation, so did the prototype of man, and as the universe evolved, so did
man evolve.

And, as man is still evolving, so is the universe still evolving, and man's evolution contributes to the universe's evolution because everything is interconnected through the field of our origin. Jack Hawk and associates at the University of Wisconsin have shown that human evolution is speeding up. According to their HapMap project, "our genes are evolving 30 to 40 times faster than they were several years ago." (Brown, 2008)

That may be a most difficult intellectual challenge, but note that we are not writing that the universe is God. (When we use the word *God*, we are not referring to any specific religious concept, but to the unknowable Creator, the ultimate divinity manifesting both within man and universe, and without, beyond or behind all manifestation.) We can know nothing of God other than what has become manifest. God is both within and without the universe, and within and without man. We are divine within but we are not divinity itself. We grow in our divinity. Our destiny is not to become divinity, but to become one with divinity, to merge back into the Source.

Quantum theory as well as the ancient wisdom teaches us that at various levels of consciousness we are connected with one another, and with the energy of the universe itself. We can use intentional thought to introduce change into the subatomic potentials in the process of becoming real. Our studies of parapsychology have also demonstrated that the ability of people to communicate with one another in a range of ways—telepathy, clairvoyance, and healing—involves the communication of energies as well as information.

We also learned that the universe communicates with us. At our moment of birth, the matrix of energies that is uniquely ours takes on a characteristic imprint from the planetary configuration at our birth time in relation to our birthplace. We call the science that has evolved from that knowledge astrology—also known as astrobiology and cosmobiology; it is applied astronomy. At any time, those communications continue and resonate in certain ways with the birth horoscope to modify the initial energy field.

But we are not merely inhabitants of a material universe enjoying various connections to the rest of the cosmos; we are actually broadcasting as well as receiving information and energies with people, animals, and parts of the universe as well. As we are residents and citizens of our own planet; we are residents and citizens of the physical universe and of the all-comprehensive cosmos.

We see stars and planets, we experience the sun and the moon daily, and we walk upon the surface of our own planet; we read about discoveries of distant galaxies and of previously unknown planets that may be home to life as we know it; and we watch spectacular dramas such as *Star Trek, Stargate,* and *Star Wars* that stir the imagination and expose us to ideas like teleportation, energy healing, mind-melding (presumably a form of mental telepathy), *The Force,* and subatomic energy conversion for space travel. But we have much to learn about the invisible universe that corresponds with the invisible parts of the human being.

When we refer to the invisible aspects of anything, we already suffer from misperception. When we speak of *mind* and *feeling* we know that we can't see thoughts and emotions, nor when we speak of *spirit* do we generally expect to see things. The images we see in our dreams and imagination are not treated as real in the same way that this book is.

Earlier we wrote that the whole person is made up of several bodies, or dimensions: physical, etheric, astral, mental, and spiritual, as well as other concepts such as self and soul. We also speak of subconscious, conscious, and superconscious; and we acknowledge the Divine within.

We are more familiar with the invisible than we may have thought. It is here with us, within us, and around us. Just as we acknowledge the invisible parts of the whole human person, we need to acknowledge the invisible parts of the universe. Quantum theory tells us that everything is fundamentally collections of subatomic packets of energy and hence everything, no matter how physical it is, is essentially various forms of energy and vibrations manifesting in various ways that may include not only matter as we know it, but matter that is also more subtle and experienced in different ways.

One problem we have is that we are uncertain about what to identify as real. If you happen to drop this book on your bare toe, you will experience one kind of reality. It is physical reality. If you grab hold of bare energized electrical wires you will experience a different kind of physical reality. And if you breathe in chlorine gas you will, at least for a short time, experience yet another kind of physical reality. Even the physical world, or the metaphysical term plane has several kinds of reality, some of which are invisible, but they are not part of the invisible universe we will be discussing.

At this point, however, we wish to make a statement: *Not all paranormal phenomena are psychic!* Remember that paranormal means beyond or beside the normal. There can be truly bizarre phenomena for which we have no explanation and which might even be invisible to the physical eye, but are actually within the physical plane. One familiar example is that of magnetism, where the magnetic field is invisible until made visible in the science lab with iron filings sprinkled on a piece of paper.

We will discuss this further, but there are phenomena that may or may not be psychic (more likely not).

When you feel love toward a person, you enter a different world, even though that other person has a physical body and your love may include the physical expression of sexual contact. Here we have an example of a physical experience enriched by an emotional experience, or you can also say that the emotional experience of love was given substance by the physical sexual expression. For the fun of it, let's further speculate that you sincerely believe that the person you love is your soul mate, and that you and she or he have been together in other lives. Now we have a still greater range of perceptions, which you still consider to be real. They are part of your reality, even if not equally perceived by others in the same way this physical book or your sore toe can be readily experienced.

When you dream, what of those images is real? When you imagine characters in the novel you are writing, what of them is real? When you have mental contact with another person, what of that is real? If you see an angel, and no one else does, what part of that experience is real?

What if you are a woman who dreams that she is pregnant, and that the baby will be a boy whose name—given in the dream—is David; what of that dream is real? To take that same dream a bit further, you go to the doctor, who confirms you are pregnant—do you then presume it is a boy? And when the baby is born and turns out to be a boy, do you feel you have to name him David? What if instead of a boy you deliver twin girls? And, maybe, still later, they each marry men named David?

In all these examples, *your reality is mostly a matter of choice*. And, sometimes, physical reality is also a matter of choice. Many of us have seen, and some have actually experienced, situations that others may consider unbelievable—such as the person who walks on white-hot coals and emerges without burns. It happens. But what if the next person to walk on these same hot coals gets burned? Most instances of this sort happen when the individual is in an *alternate state of consciousness* induced by hypnosis, religious ecstasy, drumming, mind-altering substances, or self-hypnosis. At some point, all of these different inductions involved choice. In some sense, even with the influence of drugs, every one of them is some kind of self-hypnosis. Two different people: one gets burned, the other doesn't. Each chose their own reality, consciously or not.

Another lesson from quantum theory is that, at the subatomic level, everything is either energy or matter, but we also learned that anything that is matter is really information and that anything that is information is some form of energy. But we have also learned—$E=mc^2$—that all matter can be released into energy, losing its information. That information is erased, sort of like book burning during times of religious and political oppression.

If reality, or its perception, is a matter of choice, then it is true that we generally need to match up a level of consciousness with a level, or plane, of the universe to be able to perceive and actually act upon a particular reality experienced on that plane. The doorway to these alternate levels is through the subconscious mind.

As a physical person, another physical person with a real physical baseball bat can inflict very real physical damage. Yet, perhaps you dream the very same scenario, but no damage to your physical body happens. Two different levels do not normally interact. However, if we go down to the more primitive level, intentional thought and actions expressing that thought can, when focused on the logical steps of a process, bring about change originating on one level and culminating on another.

All of this requires certain expertise and knowledge of the levels and planes so that you can select your level and apply it to the appropriate plane.

LEVELS OF CONSCIOUSNESS

There are many different models for both humankind and the universe, and each is meaningful, but each also has special pertinence depending on the ways the user will be applying it. We're especially interested in just three of these models—that of the Kabbalah, Analytical Psychology, and Western Esotericism. And of these three, we're focusing primarily just on the psychological and the esoteric in this book, as their terminology is more familiar to most readers.

The curious thing to remember is that particular terminology is pertinent to the application. Just as there are many common English words that actually change meanings depending on the context in which they are used, that is often even truer in the case of specialized applications in science and the professions. In astrology, for example, a House is not a home, and a Sign is not a short message. In astronomy, occult has nothing to do with magic or the supernatural. In hypnosis, a subject is a person, not a course of study.

While this seeming indefiniteness may induce initial confusion, its advantage is that we are forced to look at things from a multitude of perspectives and develop our own conception of the various ideas discussed. It means that we *think* more as we work with these various definitions that sometimes will appear again in association with a different word. As someone once said, the question is more important than the answer because it means you are thinking.

THE PSYCHOLOGICAL PERSPECTIVE

Mind

To borrow from the esoteric for the moment, the mind consists of the etheric, astral, and mental bodies functioning together, as personality, both through the physical brain and independently. The mind is not so much a *something* as it is a process that functions in a variety of ways that have been classified as follows:

Conscious Mind

Also called the ego, the conscious mind is the home of what we commonly refer to as consciousness. Nevertheless it is but one of several forms as will be discussed both here and below. The point is that normal consciousness is only a small portion of the total consciousness theoretically available to us dependent upon growth, training, development, and specialized techniques such as meditation and hypnosis.

It is, however, the awake and aware conscious mind, the ego, that is the rational mind *potentially in charge* of the entire complex. It is the actions, the decisions, and the willed intentions of the conscious mind that enable change, growth, and the assertion of our innate creativity. Whether inspired by the higher consciousness or prodded by the subconsciousness, it is by the processing of the conscious mind that direct physical-plane action takes place.

Subconscious Mind

Also known as the id, the unconscious mind, and the personal unconscious, the subconscious mind is inclusive of the shadow, and the anima or animus. The subconscious is the doorway to the astral.

The word unconscious describes a situation of unawareness, or not being consciously aware. We spend approximately one-third of our life asleep and it is here that we normally are in contact with the subconscious mind. The subconscious contains lost or buried memories that can be recalled in meditation and under hypnosis (and in self-hypnosis), and has the strange ability to override perceptions and sensations of the conscious mind. The subconscious can solve problems and carry on research projects as directed in meditation or under self-hypnosis.

The lost or suppressed memories make up the *shadow*. Under hypnosis and self-hypnosis, and in deep meditation and active imagination, the subconscious is able to telepathically access other subconscious minds and, to some extent, the collective unconscious where we may perceive the archetypes and gain understanding of our particular interaction with them, and possibly change those interactions from a childish to a more mature level.

In addition to the shadow, the unconscious contains the anima or animus, which is an aspect of self representing the opposite sex, an image often influencing the conscious experience and relationship with a person of the opposite sex and even more often unconscious reactions and sexual drives.

The unconscious mind is also the possible source of various entities contacted in channeling.

The conscious mind and the unconscious mind, together, are the lower self, while the superconscious mind is the higher self. Our goal is to link the two together in wholeness. *It is through the unconscious that we access the superconscious mind.*

Superconscious Mind

The superconscious mind is the higher consciousness or self able to access the collective unconscious. It is the source of inspiration, ideals, ethical behavior, and heroic action. It is the place of illumination. Direct and continual awareness of the superconscious mind is known as self-realization.

The collective unconscious is a kind of group mind that is inherited from all our ancestors and includes all the memories and knowledge acquired by humans. Nevertheless, access to the collective unconscious seems to progress from individual memories to universal memories as the person progresses in his or her spiritual development and integration of the whole being. There is some suggestion that this progression also moves from individual memories through various groups or small collectives—family, tribe, race, and nation—so that each level is reflected in consciousness until the individual progresses to join in group consciousness with all humanity. At its most advanced level, it corresponds to the cosmic consciousness experienced by Richard Bucke.

This would seem to account for some of the variations of the universal archetypes each person encounters in life.

Personality

The personality, or lower self, is a projection of the superconscious mind, or higher self, and consists of the etheric, astral, and lower mental bodies functioning *partly* through the brain. It is as personality that our consciousness expresses itself in the material world.

THE ESOTERIC PERSPECTIVE

Physical Body

Considered as our first body.

The physical and etheric bodies together correspond to the physical plane. The physical and etheric bodies die, but the consciousness moves on with the astral body.

Etheric Body

Considered as our second body.

The etheric body is the vital form behind the physical body and is sometimes considered to be an extension of the physical body and other times as a sub-level of the astral body. In either view, it is seen as a layer of the aura between the physical body and the astral. It is described as an *energy* body and other times as the *health* aura. In appearance it is seen clairvoyantly as a silver-gray layer of fine "needles" of energy. In good health, the needles should be vibrant and straight; in ill health, they lose their vibrancy and often lose their straightness over injured or diseased parts of the physical body.

The etheric body channels subtle energy (Prana) from the cosmos to the physical body. Some diseases relate to a temporary or even semi-permanent lack of exact coincidence between the physical and etheric bodies. Some abilities involving extreme sensitivity of any of the senses relate to particular developments in the etheric body.

Ill health having its origin in the physical body shows up first in the etheric body. Energy therapies such as acupuncture, Reiki, homeopathy, and nonphysical techniques work primarily at the etheric level and then work down into the physical body.

Upon death of the physical body, the etheric body dies too—sometimes taking as little as three days and other times longer.

Astral Body

Considered as our third body.

The astral body is also called the mortal soul, the subtle body, the *ba*, the emotional or desire body, and the dream body, as it is there that we experiences dreams. It is also the seat of memory and relates to the mental body in this respect. The astral body eventually dies and consciousness moves on to the mental body.

As the emotional body, it is emotions themselves that determine its nature and our psychological health. Strong negative emotions are injurious and can even harm the physical body. Strong positive emotions, when directed under mind and will, can heal and even change physical reality. It is the power of emotion that can reach down into the universal subatomic field, or matrix, and create new realities.

Emotion presents a paradox: it is calmness and clarity that allow psychic phenomena to be experienced—telepathy, clairvoyance, clairaudience, psychometry, etc.—but it is with emotion that psychic phenomena such as telekinesis and healing can be brought about. In either case there has to be clarity of mind and purpose. We have to be free of mental clutter and chatter, of emotional baggage, fear, and doubt. And we need to learn to distinguish between emotion, feeling, and belief.

Emotion is energy. *E-motion* is energy in motion that is the source of magical powers. Feelings are sensitivities to astral currents. Belief is your personal operating system that frames all your emotions and your unique perception of reality. For some, it is experienced as faith.

The astral body is the main center for psychic skills and paranormal phenomena. In general, all nonhuman entities have been called spirits, and they are primarily experienced on the astral plane, These include spirit guides or guardian spirit, spirits of the recently deceased in transition to higher realms, elementals, angels, demons, thought forms, etc. In other words, it's a catch-all classification for which we will try to provide some definition.

It is the astral body that can separate from the physical in out-of-body experiences. During separation, they are joined by a cord of subtle energy/matter usually called the "silver cord."

Thought forms are astral images or mental concepts that take on a seemingly objective reality with a life of their own. The characters created in a novelist's mind become real enough to speak and spin their own tales for the writer. Thought forms can be given even greater reality when empowered through ritual or energized with strong emotion. When ritually empowered, they are charged with specific missions, such as functioning as a household guardian or a personal familiar, or given specific assignments at the conclusion of which they should be ritually discharged and the image disbursed—otherwise it can take on further objectivity and become an independent and destructive entity.

As mental concepts, they are like a blueprint or plan around which related thoughts coalesce.

Mental Body

Considered as our fourth body.

The lower mental body is combined with the physical and etheric/astral bodies to form the personality while the higher mental body is home to the soul between incarnations.

Spiritual Body, or Spirit

Considered as our fifth body, the term is sometimes used loosely to include all the nonphysical bodies, but here we define it and give it structure. It is also known as the divine spark, ego, and *monad,* and further includes the causal body and the Atman.

Causal Body

Also known as *manas,* or abstract mind, the intuitional body, as well as Buddhi, higher cosmic intelligence, and spiritual awareness.

Considered as our sixth body. It is the source of wisdom.

Atmic Body

Or Atman, the eternal self, the overself, the soul which incarnates but does not directly participate in the individual life which it observes, and can access all its previous incarnations.

Considered as our seventh body. It is the source of the will.

Soul

The soul consists of the higher mental body and monad. It is also known as Atman, the higher self, Neshamah, the Ka, and level of Christ consciousness. The higher self is the divinity within, and is above and beyond the personality. It is unaffected by the physical body or the personality.

There is a gap between soul and personality (the lower self of physical, astral, and the lower mental bodies), and it is the work of the personality and the soul to construct the "rainbow bridge" to close this gap, linking the personality and the higher self. This is the process of self-knowledge.

This is also known as "the Great Work" of all self-development programs—whether we think in terms of psychological, spiritual, yogic, tantric, or other systems, including those historic paths of alchemy, shamanism, Wicca, occultism, etc. The work is that of growing the personality into the whole person, into becoming aware on those levels other than physical we've been talking about—etheric, astral, mental, and spiritual. The work is to become self-directed at the level of the higher self, the soul.

This work of personal growth and development is the continuation of human evolution, no longer limited to that of the species but as personal and self-directed. The work is our responsibility—each and every one of us. It is the meaning of life, the great purpose each of us has.

This work, the great purpose we each have, is the process of growth and development and it is accomplished by making awareness part of everything you do. A purposeful life is not limited to great humanitarian projects or selfless dedication to community welfare or service to the poor, the helpless, the sick and needy. It is doing all work well and feeling the broad effect of what you are doing, not just in terms of others but also in terms of yourself. Nearly any job becomes your great work through realization of the process and acceptance of the responsibility you have to grow. Expanding your awareness is the process, and it also becomes a great adventure as you begin seeing and feeling at these additional levels until you can function consciously on all levels all the time *even as the physical body sleeps.*

It's not that these are higher levels—although from another perspective they are—but that your expanding awareness brings a broader vision of the levels of your consciousness and the levels of the universe around you to which you are connected. Your physical body is part of the physical plane, your astral body is part of the astral plane, your mental body is part of the mental plane, and each of these is a magnificent world.

This work is also the continued evolution of the universe, the cosmos, the macrocosm. You are the microcosm and you are part of the macrocosm. As above, so below; as within, so without. Your evolution is evolutionary to the universe because you are part of it. Our origins are shared and our destiny is shared. *We*—all life and all we see and all that we don't as yet see—*are family. Love is the bridge that unites all.*

STATES OF CONSCIOUSNESS

So far we been discussing *levels,* or bodies of consciousness, but in bridging between above and below, inner and outer, we do so through states of consciousness. However, it is also pertinent to our discussion to consider the aura and chakras.

Aura

The physical body is surrounded by a colorful energy field that is constantly changing, reflecting the person's health and feelings. It usually extends from the body for about eighteen inches, and is made up of all the different bodies beyond the physical, and is the interface between the individual and the universe.

Clairvoyants read the aura much as astrologers read the horoscope, interpreting the colors in specific relation to a person's emotions. Most psychic perception is limited to the etheric and astral levels, and hence may not reflect the mental or higher levels.

Chakras

These are energy centers, or gates, that transfer cosmic energies to the body and power to the psyche. While their name and number vary with the tradition, the most common number is seven as in both the Hindu and Kabbalist traditions. The most familiar names and associations are taken from the Hindu and popularized by Theosophy.

They are important to this discussion, if only to recognize that with our growth and development, successive chakras are activated in turn.

There are five basic states of consciousness: awareness, dream sleep, dreamless sleep, coma, and trance—otherwise considered as an alternative state of consciousness. There may be several such states, providing for specific communication or access, sometimes described as "channel." We have already discussed awareness and dreams; dreamless sleep and coma are not pertinent to this book.

Trance

The trance state is one of the most unusual and most interesting, seeming to vary between half-awake to the external environment to being focused totally elsewhere. It can be induced by external circumstance—through hypnosis, shamanic practices, religious fervor, guided meditation, heavy music, hallucinogenic drugs, monotonous repetition of stimuli, and sensory deprivation with no external stimuli.

It can also be self-induced, through self-hypnosis, deep meditation, the use of a crystal ball or magic mirror, extreme exercise as in running, breathing exercises, rhythmic chanting, and personal rituals, often involving sensory overload, including sexual practices.

Trance functions as a doorway to the subconscious mind.

The **Hypnotic Trance** is an induced loss of personal consciousness with enhanced suggestibility that can be used to bring about changes in physiology, recall of lost memories, and various forms of psychic phenomena. All hypnosis is self-hypnosis because the person to be hypnotized can—if aware—withhold permission to be hypnotized. Still, a professional hypnotist may be able to induce deeper levels of hypnosis until a person becomes trained in self-hypnosis.

Through the hypnotic trance, as the chatter of ordinary consciousness is reduced, your powers of concentration are enhanced and subconscious memories and perceptions are brought to awareness. An important part of induced, or guided, hypnosis is the controlled use of the imagination.

During the **Mediumistic Trance**, the personality seems to step aside, allowing another entity or fragment of the personality to occupy and use the body of the individual who then serves as a medium, or is ridden as a horse in Voudoun. During this trance, the medium is usually unaware of behavior or speech. In these and other trance states there sometimes are various paranormal phenomena, some of which may be spontaneous occurrences and others occur as the result of direction from a person or entity acting as a *control*.

In a **Shamanic Trance,** the shaman enters areas of the astral plane to gain knowledge through observation and communication with astral entities, and returns to ordinary awareness with full memory of the encounters.

Imagination

The imagination is a function, or channel, of the mind by which we create images. Various systems of training in magic and meditation involve developing the ability to visualize images in great detail that serve as keys to particular areas of the unconscious. Particular images have a long tradition of providing access to associated areas of the astral plane and function as keys to obtain knowledge or encounters with elementals or spirits *corresponding* to the symbol images.

The imagination also functions to channel intuitive or psychic impressions to the conscious mind.

Intuition

Intuition is awareness on the soul-level and occurs as a sudden knowledge, independent of thought. While sometimes occurring upon awakening from sleep, and other times seemingly out of nowhere, it can be a response to conscious questions directed to the subconscious mind. Intuition is believed to be a function of the brow chakra and often comes during or following intense concentration.

Inspiration

Inspiration differs from intuition in that it is more a sequence of ideas, while intuition is a single blinding insight. In addition, inspiration usually *inspires* action while intuition is more often knowledge for its own sake. Inspiration often seems to come from inner guides or entities, whereas intuition seems purely from within oneself. Inspiration is said to be associated with the throat chakra while intuition comes from the crown chakra.

PLANES OF THE UNIVERSE

Just as the *invisible* part of the human being is far more complex than "meets the eye," so is the invisible part of the universe. It is often said that we use only 10 percent of our potential while 90 percent of the universe seems to be empty space. It's that missing 90 percent in both instances that is the concern of this book.

There is an important distinction to be made here: even with the physical universe, we know there is much that is invisible to the naked eye that becomes visible with the aid of sophisticated microscopes and electronic devices. Physicists also tell of subatomic and even smaller levels not yet visible by these means that are inferred because of the evidence produced in physical observation and experimentation. Even these levels are still part of the physical universe and not the invisible world, which we will be considering next.

The invisible world is, in some ways, more real than the visible world, which is a reflection of the inner reality.

The inner planes are more like nonspatial dimensions than layers of space. It is important for our discussion to accept the concept that *whatever eventually manifests in the physical world is first conceived and born (becoming a micro matrix) on one of these higher levels and progressively travels from higher to lower, picking up substance from each.* It is thus that precognition is able to perceive the shadows from the future.

It is also true that this progression from higher to lower and inner to outer can be changed, interrupted, and even disrupted prior to its materialization. *The future may exist now, but it can also be changed now.*

Earlier we discussed three levels of consciousness: Super, or higher, consciousness; middle, or ordinary conscious awareness; and lower, or subconsciousness. It is important to realize that models of consciousness correspond or connect us with models of the universe. In old European mythology, the world or universe is divided into three levels:

Asgard, the higher world where the gods live. Access to Asgard is possible only by the Rainbow Bridge.

Midgard, the middle world where humans live.

Nifelheim, the lower world, or *Hel*, the underworld.

This same pattern is common to many mythologies, and should be seen in the light of three levels of consciousness we found in the psychological perspective reviewed earlier. The point is that reality is experienced both inwardly and outwardly, one as the reflection of the other.

In the esoteric perspective, we perceived seven bodies of consciousness, and these seven levels are likewise seen as seven planes of the universe.

BEFORE THERE WAS SOMETHING, THERE WAS NOTHING

At least nothing of which we can have any knowledge or understanding. *And then there was something.* With the origin of the universe there came the **Subatomic Level,** also called ether and the field. It is the source of all, and through it we are all joined together. We also call it the **Matrix,** an organizing principle behind the process of manifestation.

"... the Divine Matrix (is) ... (1) the container for the universe to exist within; (2) the bridge between our inner and outer worlds; and (3) the mirror that reflects our everyday thoughts, feelings, emotions, and beliefs." In addition, it is everywhere all the time. It originated when creation did, with the big bang, the beginning. It has intelligence and responds to the power of human emotion" (Bradden, 54–55).

Everything we say in this book is understood in relation to this concept of the Field or Matrix. As humans, we remain in contact with the Field, and through it our thoughts and emotions are vehicles for whatever reality we perceive.

THE SEVEN ESOTERIC PLANES

Physical or Etheric Plane

Considered as the first level, it is also called *Adi*. This is the plane of our visible universe and what we perceive as ordinary reality.

The physical and etheric bodies together correspond to the physical plane. Time and distance are phenomena of the material or physical plane, but not of higher levels.

Astral Plane

Considered as the second level. Also called the emotional plane, Bardo, *Kamaloca, Anapadaka,* and the psychic plane. The astral plane can also be considered as a parallel universe to the physical.

There are seven subplanes to each plane, and it is from the lowest subplane of the astral closest to the physical world that most spiritual communications originate. The higher a spirit's evolutionary state, the more difficult it is for such communication. More advanced spirits quickly move on to the mental plane or Heaven-world.

The astral plane contains imagery from the unconscious mind and is home to most recorded psychic and occult phenomena, including various inhabitants such as guides, elementals, nature spirits, elves, fairies, demons, and entities created in the imagination, especially out of fear. It is also the world of the imagination where objects and beings we visualize take shape, including those charged with emotion. Thought forms are created by magicians out of the astral light, and charged with instructions to carry out certain operations. Some thought forms are believed to be karmic, of past life origin, that appear in the etheric body in the current life to repercuss into the physical until exhausted or transmuted by conscious healing of the causal relationship.

It is also said to be the home of the Akashic records, where every memory is recorded, and often experienced as a great library providing access to every kind of information. It should be noted that the Akashic records are also said to be located on the mental plane, but it may be that such resources exist on both levels.

It is on the astral plane that we may encounter those nature spirits that rule nonhuman life including those associated with the four elements of Earth (gnomes, trolls, kobolds, dwergers), Water (undines, mermaids, nereides, nayads), Fire (salamanders), and Air (sylphs, brownies, elves, pixies). Other spiritual rulers include fauns and satyrs for animal life and dryads for vegetable life.

Among psychic phenomenon encounters on the etheric/astral plane is the poltergeist, which originates in repressed emotions and the loose psychic energy of puberty.

It is also the place where Earth forces can be perceived. These may include the following:

The **Morphogenetic Field,** proposed by Rupert Sheldrake as a field surrounding all living organisms and connecting them in harmonic association so that when one of a class—such as monkeys on one island—learns something new and valuable, it is soon copied by other monkeys on that island, and then transferred by Morphic Resonance to other monkeys elsewhere.

The **Life Field,** proposed by Prof. Harold Burr as a matrix of electric-like energy surrounding all living organisms and holding each to its shape even as the cells and molecules are always being replaced through life's wear and tear.

The **Psychic Blueprint,** proposed by Sir Alister Hardy to function in relation to a psychic stream of information flowing between members of a species.

The **Subtle Fluid,** posited by Mesmer to pervade the universe and associate all things in a kind of magnetic relationship.

The **Biosphere,** proposed by Pierre Teilhard de Chardin as the domain of all organic life on our planet.

Orgone, proposed by Wilhelm Reich as a life force everywhere in the universe.

Odic Force, proposed by Baron Karl von Reichenbach as a force pervading all nature and radiating from all objects and bodies.

Prana, or life force, existing everywhere in the universe. Also called Mana, Ch'i, and Baraka.

The **Psi-Field,** posited by G. D. Wassermann to surround all objects.

Psychotronic Energy, posited by Robert Pavlita as the power behind psychic phenomena.

Radionic Energy is the source of radiation detected in dowsing work. Radionic detection seems dependent both on the use of an instrument, such as a pendulum, and the person holding the instrument.

Shakti, the feminine life-activating principle.

Astral projection, astral travel, and out-of-body experiences are names for the phenomena of consciousness separating from the physical body either with full awareness and response to willed directions or during sleep. Some dreams may be encounters with astral beings.

While the general belief is that the astral body actually moves out of alignment with the physical and travels in the astral world, able to observe and interact with the physical world at distant location, some people speculate that such seeming *external* astral experiences are really internal, a form of astral imagination. However, external and internal may be the same given that the astral body and the astral plane are of the same substance and having laws different than those of the physical world.

Mental Plane

Considered as the third level, also called the causal plane, the noetic, or *Atmic*.

This is the heaven-world for most souls in between lives where the whole of life can be understood. It is also the plane where we may encounter saints and angels as well as members of our family.

It may also constitute the noosphere of Pierre Teilhard de Chardin, a network of thought surrounding the earth connecting all of humanity and through which we share our mental life of intellectual discovery and artistic culture.

Intuitional Plane

Considered as the fourth level, also called *Buddhic*.

This is the highest plane most people can reach. It is the plane of mystical experience, and the plane where we encounter great teachers sometimes called Masters.

Spiritual Plane

Considered as the fifth level, also called *Nirvanic,* or the third heaven, and home to the Holy Spirit, Brahma.

Monadic Plane

Considered as the sixth level, also called *Manasic,* and home to Christ, Archangels, Vishnu.

Divine Plane

Considered as the seventh level, home to God the Father.

If there is a Beyond, it is as unknowable as before the beginning.

HOW IT ALL COMES TOGETHER

We've spent a lot of time merely describing a particular model of the cosmos. Our goal is psychic empowerment, and what we've attempted to show is that everything we mean by this involves our expansion of awareness to the whole person, and an understanding of the whole universe. As Gregg Bradden put it: "To tap the force of the universe itself, we must see ourselves as *part* of the world rather than *separate from* it." (Bradden, 12)

To be empowered is to move from passive victimization to positive participation. What Bradden and quantum scientists are saying is essentially that the *universe is participatory, and is constantly responding to consciousness.* Through human emotion we can intentionally bring about change by reaching into the non-local, holographic, universal energy field. "… our connection to the field is the essence of our existence. If we understand how it works and the way we're connected to it, then we have all that we need to apply what we know of the field to our lives." (Bradden, 53)

To be empowered, our understanding must fully become part of our belief system, which is the operating system through which we feel and act. We have to substitute this new view—a view that combines quantum theory with the ancient wisdom of East and West—for the divisive and belittling view of the person common to our world today. We have to *grow up* and accept a new role as co-creators of our reality and bring others into that realization in order to provide sufficient power to change the shared common reality. That's the ultimate meaning of change in today's landscape of crisis and pain.

Before we leave this discussion of levels and planes, we want to refer to another trinity, that of self-consciousness, group consciousness, and God consciousness. Each is an obvious stage of progression as we extend our awareness to comprehend yet greater dimensions. Can we actually progress to a state of God consciousness? Can we even define what is meant by this? If we accept the concept of continued evolution, don't we have to accept such a goal—that each unit progresses to encompass other units? It's food for meditation.

PARALLEL UNIVERSES
AND ALTERNATE DIMENSIONS

Earlier we suggested that the astral plane could be considered to be a parallel universe, or even as parallel universes.

Physicists and mathematicians, as well as science-fiction writers, have long speculated about such parallel universes that somehow exist beyond our astronomical universe. As such, they are not seen as additional dimensions or levels, but as separate and truly alternate realities undoubtedly inaccessible to any but the highest consciousness.

But the astral plane offers enormous possibilities within our own astronomical universe while outside our familiar range of consciousness.

THE LOCH NESS MONSTER, UFOS, AND
OTHER DISAPPEARING PHENOMENA

There are so many instances of seeming paranormal phenomena on a large scale—ranging from UFOs to incredible beings such as the Loch Ness Monster, from phantom aircraft and ships to inexplicable happenings of the nature of the Philadelphia Experiment in which a U.S. Navy ship is claimed to have disappeared and then reappeared as the result of electromagnetic distortion, and the weirdness of the Bermuda Triangle—that many people speculate on the idea of alternative dimensions or a parallel universe from which and into which these things occasionally slip between one reality and another.

Rather than being psychic phenomena, it is more likely that the Philadelphia Experiment involved extreme physical energies as suggested by Joseph Farrell in *Secrets of the Unified Field*. There still is debate as to whether UFOs are physical objects powered by similar extreme energies, or a particular class of psychic phenomena. Either way, they remain a legitimate object of paranormal research until the question is resolved.

WATER, FIRE, EARTH, AND AIR

Equally feasible is a psychic perspective in which powerful images and entities from the astral plane may take on enough etheric substance to temporarily appear in places and to people where the layer between the physical and astral thins out, just as it does with ectoplasmic substance during spiritualist séances. The Loch Ness Monster and other creatures seem more likely to be astral in origin and we might look to their geographic homes for clues on their origin and activity. Bodies of water do seem to be associated with otherworldly creatures.

Similarly, certain other dimensional creatures are associated with volcanoes and Fire, others are associated with caves and Earth, and others with Air and windy mountainous areas.

It is legitimate to consider all of these as paranormal phenomena until we understand what energies are involved. Psychic investigation of such phenomena may lead to such understanding for the simple reason that the psychic perspective is broader and is inclusive of physical as well as etheric and astral energies.

We live in a beautiful and wondrous universe, and we are part of it. Welcome to the great new adventure of your psychic growth with which your perceptions will expand and your spirit will soar.

References

Alice Bailey, *The Consciousness of the Atom* (New York: Lucis, 1961).

Gregg Bradden, *The Divine Matrix—Bridging Time, Space, Miracles, and Belief* (Carlsbad, CA: Hay House, 2007).

Arnold Brown, "The New Biology Paradigm" (*The Futurist*, September–October, 2008).

Richard M. Bucke, *Cosmic Consciousness* (New York: Dutton, 1923).

Joseph P. Farrell, *Secrets of the Unified Field—The Philadelphia Experiment, the Nazi Bell, and the Discarded Theory* (Kempton, IL: Adventures Unlimited Press, 2008).

Joseph C. Pearce, *The Crack in the Cosmic Egg* (New York: Julian Press, 1971).

Donald Watson, *The Dictionary of Mind and Spirit* (New York: Avon Books, 1991).

CHAPTER TEN

EMBRACING AND EMPOWERING THE GLOBE
Addressing Global Problems and Needs

It was the best of times, it was the worst of times,
It was the age of wisdom, it was the age of foolishness,
It was the epoch of belief, it was the epoch of incredulity,
It was the season of Light, it was the season of Darkness,
It was the spring of hope, it was the winter of despair,
We had everything before us, we had nothing before us,
We were all going direct to Heaven, we were all going direct
    the other way.
                    —Charles Dickens, *A Tale of Two Cities*, 1859

THE CHALLENGES OF THESE TIMES

Charles Dickens' words about the French Revolution could be as easily said about the times in which we now live. An unknown person said, "These times, they are dangerous." We commonly perceive news events as dangerous more often than we welcome them as opportunity, and yet both are always present in some proportion—sometimes favoring one over the other.

But these are probably more dangerous and challenging times for all humanity than any before in known history. And yet, we have enormous opportunities, not only for the positive resolution of these challenges, but the option to apply the most recent scientific knowledge concerning psychic powers to common reality.

It doesn't matter whether you live in North America or in another part of the world, the challenges we all face are enormous, and from a mundane perspective the chances for peace, prosperity, and what we like to call progress seem less than comfortable. At the time of this writing, we are still waiting to see how the famous Mayan prophecy of the *End of the World (at least as we know it)* on December 21, 2012, works out. Of course, the tempering phrase *"as we know it"* offers a tremendous hedge. Tomorrow is always different than yesterday.

And we are optimists. We believe we will be here to celebrate a new year in January 2013. And we believe that not only will we survive but we will see a new beginning with the passing of the old age. Nevertheless, we cannot be complacent; we cannot just assume that *"the best is yet to come."* We humans have intervened in the natural order too much and now have to recognize the repercussions of our disturbance and make necessary changes for our very survival. We have to do our part to change old ways to new ways.

A simple listing of challenges at the time of this writing includes all of the following:

- Global warming and climate change, melting ice caps, endangered species
- Increasing incidences of extreme weather, hurricanes, tornados, droughts, floods, tsunamis
- Increasing incidences and severity of earthquakes, volcanic eruptions, and other earth changes
- The energy crisis of impending fossil fuel shortages, and inadequate and delayed development of alternative fuels
- Periodic shortages of nearly all natural resource commodities, with resultant high prices of food and manufactured goods leading to inflation and economic distortions
- The worldwide credit crisis and loss of confidence in national and global financial institutions leading to deflation and collapsing economies

- International terrorism combined with religious fanaticism, the spread of powerful weapons that can be triggered by individuals or small groups, and the collapse of democratic governments

- The reappearance of nationalist expansionism and tribal/ethnic conflicts causing extensive suffering and death to minority populations

- The seeming renewal of the Cold War between resurgent Russia and the overextended United States, with a near helpless Europe in the middle

- A very real arms race, with arms producers again selling weaponry to all comers

- The existence of, and newly emerging threats of, nuclear blackmail

- The appearance and spread of new diseases through rapid migration of people and importation of animal and vegetable products beyond their natural habitat

- The potential danger of dependence on newly deployed technology without redundancy for backup and shortages of trained personnel

- A failing educational system not providing even basic skills of the information age for a technology-based culture, economy, and a global society

- Rapid technological change and innovation in e-commerce that undermine status quo bricks-and-mortar businesses

- Failures in government to adequately meet the legal challenges of changed knowledge and communication industries

- A crumbling infrastructure of transportation, utilities, communications, and public safety

- The loss of ethical, moral, and spiritual pertinence to guide individual and institutional behavior

- The lack of true international law and an enforceable justice system

- The growth of piracy—on the high seas, on the Internet, and in the marketplace through noncompliance with copyright and trademark laws, evasions of patent protection, and blatant theft of intellectual property
- An inability to develop a supportive, nonpunitive tax system
- The lack of meaningful and pertinent political debate
- Failed, fiscally irresponsible governments administered by ideologues and special interests
- The failure of democratic and parliamentary governments to address the fundamental needs of their constituencies rather than pandering to superficialities and special interests
- A worldwide lack of sufficient investment in new technologies and basic science

The list could go on and on. It's like the drumbeat of disaster, the sound of a failing heart, or the whine of an incoming missile.

Yes, these should be seen as dangerous times, but most people turn their heads and instead play electronic games and listen to their I-Pods, absorb themselves in the glamour of steroid-enhanced athletes and silicone-endowed entertainers, and eat themselves into dangerous obesity and diabetes. Schools are teaching religious fundamentalism at the expense of science and problem-solving methodologies; replacing science and math courses with athletic programs for the few at the expense of the many; and replacing sex education with sex ignorance and social ineptitude.

THE END TIMES AND 2012

Are these dangerous times truly the End Times prophesied by Nostradamus and others? Is any psychic prediction or prophecy absolutely determinate?

No! Think of what we have learned thus far about the nature of the pulsating field of subatomic energy packets that represent potentials and possibilities until the outcome is fixed by observation making them probabilities and realities. In the case of something possible at a future time, the final determination can only happen at the critical moment, or string of moments. Prior to that, directed, intentional, energized thought, especially when multiplied in power through group participation, can change the seemingly determinate future.

Think of what you now know of psychic powers—*your psychic power*. The psychic world is not only predictive but it can be *projective*—we have the power to change the future with enough effort and conviction. We don't just receive images from the future; we can project powerful, superimposing change-empowered images into the future to overlay those older images from another time. You, we, can prevent Armageddon, no matter who predicted it.

PEACE, PROSPERITY, AND PROGRESS FOR 2013: A POSITIVE PROGRAM WE CAN DO

We can take positive actions in regard to every one of that long litany of challenges described earlier. And we can also condense all those challenges into a single comprehensive counter-formula of peace, prosperity, and progress, and condense that into a single powerful *sigil*: PPP. But, we have to put a time tag onto that. Regardless of our belief in the Mayan date line of 2012, we can image peace, prosperity and progress for 2013.

PPP—2013

What if everyone reading this book goes into daily meditation or prayer and images **PPP—2013**, knowing that it represents an end to the troubled present world as we know it, the one filled with potential disasters represented by the long list of challenges, and replaces it with a new beginning of **PPP—2013**, a genuine New Order of the Ages as promised in the great seal of the United State of America, *Novus Ordo Seclorum?*

Let's take everything we learn through this book, and along with all the other practical applications of our increased psychic skills, do this one simple meditation exercise to help make a better world, ushering in a real New Age of higher consciousness; an age of love and beauty; and an age of peace, prosperity and progress.

All meditation work benefits from performance in a special place that offers peace and quiet, but the wonderful thing about meditation is that you can do it anywhere at any time (but not while driving, please). The important element is YOU, not the place. And you don't have to place yourself in a challenging physical posture, although, in general, sitting is preferred to lying down for the simple reason that we too often tend to fall asleep when doing so. A recliner in half-position is a good compromise. Repetition in the same place does establish a psychic power spot that reinforces your work, the more you use it.

An important first step in meditation is to slow your brain waves down to the alpha level, which roughly corresponds to what used to be called a "brown study," suited to daydreaming. To achieve this, simply close your eyes and breathe slowly and rhythmically, with the in-breath about the same length as the out-breath. Many practitioners recommend breathing in through the nose and out through the mouth, but the most important thing is to focus on breathing slowly and rhythmically, in and out, in and out. If you can work up to doing this for ten to fifteen minutes, you will have many health benefits, relieving stress, and clarifying your mind, free of emotion.

Remaining free of emotion, remaining physically and mentally relaxed, remaining poised and aware of the moment, feel yourself here and now, aware only of yourself in your body as if you are a clean slate beneath a cloudless sky.

Now, as we did previously, look within for the light that powers your whole being—body, mind, and spirit. Feeling it is the same as seeing it. Become one with the light, bathing in it and feeling refreshed, reenergized, even rejuvenated, for this light is the source of your personal life-force. Continue with this feeling, and then see and feel your personal force as part of the universal force field, a pulsating ocean of subatomic energy. You are filled with infinite peace, infinite harmony, and infinite power.

PPP—2013

Feeling this connection with the Source, think of our sigil: **PPP—2013**. *Feel it, see it, and know it is filled with the energy of the Source; know* *that it is empowered to bring to reality all that **PPP—2013** represents. Know, too, that you have been joined with others in bringing this into reality. Feel that our work has been joined by a Greater Force. (Continue this for about ten minutes—but don't stop to check the clock!)*

One final step: You must truly feel that you are living in a world of peace, prosperity, and progress. You are substituting a new reality for the old one, and to do that you must leave the old one and know that you are living in the new one. You are in your all-powerful subconscious mind that recognizes only images and feelings. Truly feel that you are now living in the image you have created.

Feel that we have started this process and all that it means, and then let go and slowly withdraw from the universal Source and return to your own personal source and gently return to wakefulness. Feel with certainty that we have peace, prosperity, and progress *already now. It is the new reality in process.*

Let go of this special work and return to your regular activity.

Repeat daily if you can. Doing this meditation work at approximately the same time and place is helpful, but don't become rigid in the externals because it is what you do internally that counts.

Let's review what we've done. First of all, realize that when we enter into this wonderful New World in 2013, you can continue the process by progressing the time factor to 2014, and then to 2015, etc. 2013 is just the starting point, and the work of building a brand new world must continue.

But, what have we done? We set forth the problem and detailed the challenges we face in resolving the problem. Then we developed a formula that represents the solution to these challenges as "Peace, Prosperity and Progress," and condensed all that these three words mean into a single formula, or sigil, representing the end of the old world and the start of the new. We took that sigil deep inside, through our subconscious mind, to our personal power source, and then merged into the universal Source and empowered the sigil to accomplish all that we intended. Then we placed ourselves in this new reality. And then we let go, knowing that we have set in motion the process of bringing it into reality. We let go, launching our empowered program to change the future.

It's a simple concept, and one that is adaptable to any goal—not just one that fixes problems but that brings about any positive change.

This meditation work is a process. It is not the training of your psychic skills that you are learning in this book. With trained psychic skills you bring psychic power to all you do. You can employ your psychic skills to foresee future probabilities; you can employ your psychic skills to better understand the inner workings of every project you are involved with; you can employ your psychic skills to perceive the challenges in every relationship; and you can employ your psychic skills to enrich your life in every dimension.

GLOBAL AWARENESS AND GLOBAL COMMUNICATION

For the first time in history, nearly all the peoples of the world are connected together through global awareness and global communication. Through radio and television we are almost instantly aware of events anywhere on the globe. Through the World Wide Web we can communicate with anyone anywhere. We have the potential for material-level global consciousness, as if we now, consciously, shared in our common humanity. *We are family!*

Through the universal Source, we have subatomic and molecular-level, psychic global consciousness, but in addition, we now we also have real-world global consciousness. Think of it as one human family living in one planetary home. Every day we see instances of global responsibility with care being extended from nation to nation and more importantly, from people to people. The victims of natural disasters, and man-made ones as well, are extended aid from many nations and from people everywhere.

Today we see the expanding global economy bringing prosperity to recently classified third-world countries. We see a growing middle class of educated and prosperous people in China, in India, in Brazil, and in other nations who demand their governments lead them to peace, prosperity, and progress. *No one need be left behind!*

KNOWLEDGE, KNOW-HOW, AND KULTUR

Through global communication, more people see the reality of peace, prosperity, and progress in other parts of the world, and they believe that the new reality can replace that of their old reality of deprivation, disease, and denial. Through the World Wide Web, knowledge, know-how, and kultur (kultur: the total product of human creativity and intellect, *Roget's II: The New Thesaurus*) can replace ignorance, idleness, and idolatry. With the Internet and the cell phone, e-communication, e-commerce, and e-education can replace insularity, indigence, and illiteracy.

The potential for a golden New Age is all about us. The challenges listed above can be solved if we apply ingenuity to bypass the existing dead ends. The answers and solutions are not self-evident, but the potential is known. The real challenge is how to realize the potential, by-passing special-interest lobbyists and others unwilling to take unknown trails.

For one example, the challenge of the energy crisis: The energy involved in exchanges between subatomic particles is far greater than the energy available for release from matter, and the energy in a cubic meter of space is enough to boil all the oceans of the world. (McTaggart, 12)

Yes, it's a dramatic claim, and it's a long distance from recognizing the potential to bringing it to practical application. But, according to the folklore, it was a personal note from Albert Einstein to President Franklin Roosevelt giving the formula of $E=mc^2$ that launched the program resulting in the first atomic bomb and today's nuclear power industry. *A single idea from a single person can change the world.*

To meet such challenges as we face today does require dramatic new thinking, thinking that can be augmented with the psychic skills you are learning in this book. Creativity is highly valued, and rightly so, in any profession, in any enterprise, in every situation. *Where does creativity come from?* Our *Encarta* dictionary defines creativity as "the ability to use the imagination to develop new and original ideas or things, especially in an artistic context."

Our imagination is found not in the mind but in the psychic body, and like other psychic powers it can be developed and refined as a skill the better to probe the universal field for information that can be used in moving from potential to probable to reality. It doesn't matter whether it is energy or information or new ideas, we can tap into the universal Source for our answers. And it is through your psychic skills that you accomplish this.

We can use words like intuition to describe the flashes of information we receive, and we can exercise our creativity in calling for the information we desire and need. When you follow the previously described procedure of relaxation and meditation to contact the universal Source, you can focus on a question presented as simply, yet specifically, as possible. Answers will come, rarely in immediate response but more often in gentle hints and suggestions, in expanding awareness that inspires your work to lead toward solutions to the questions and problems.

It is important that the work of reaching for answers and this work of prodding to shape the future be a regular feature of your life. What we are asking you to do is expand your awareness to comprehend your whole being. This requires training and discipline. You want to access specific bands of consciousness just as you tune in to specific bands of the television spectrum. You don't want to receive everything that is being broadcast without distinction. That would be meaningless garbage. The same is true of consciousness. Training enables you to be selective in channeling the flow of pertinent information.

We're asking you to expand your awareness in your daily activities. As you witness events around you, try to feel beyond the moment. When you look at beauty, bring it inside and let it enrich your soul. When you are enjoying a relationship, see it from the other side as well as your own. Learn to tune in to other people's feelings and ideas alongside your own. Do all of this without reaction—this is not a time to be critical or to change other people to fit your desires or convenience. Just observe, and try to extend your field of awareness to include your psychic perceptions. On the job, be aware of the *customer* (there is always a customer in every business and professional situation, even if you are not directly involved in sales work) and see both sides of the relationship with the possibilities of improvement in product or service.

As a whole person you become a more holy person, filled with spiritual essence. You are operating from a higher and more comprehending dimension of consciousness. You are evolving through your own efforts and work. You are making your own life truly meaningful.

GLOBAL CONSCIOUSNESS AND GLOBAL RESPONSIBILITY

As we enter into expanded awareness and higher conscious, as we have greater control over our psychic powers and skills, we will participate to a growing extent in the global consciousness and—hence—need to be more responsible. With increased power comes increased responsibility.

You are not only a citizen of your town or city, of your state or country, you are a citizen of the world and even more, a citizen of humanity.

The greatest wounds of humanity today arise from divisive tribalism, divisive nationalism, and divisive religious teachings. It's the "us against them"; the deliberate instillation of hatred of the other by religious and political leaders; the belief that the *other* must change to conform to *our* values and principles.

We see it in the horrors of terrorism in all the religious, political, and criminal dimensions that fill the news every day. It's the major cause for the resurgence of militarism and economic imbalances today. It's the repression of women and the use of children as thoughtless soldiers. Terrorism is war imposed by one party on others. And to proclaim it in the service of God is the height of arrogance and to follow those who do so is the abdication of intelligence and morality.

What can we do about it?

ENLIGHTENMENT, ENRICHMENT, AND EMPOWERMENT: A NEW WORLD ORDER

We have to assert our human citizenship and not respond to any such divisiveness. Self-defense is always necessary and legitimate, but pre-emptive war is not. Never let emotion guide decisions involving questions of life and death in military affairs or political debate.

As citizens of humanity, our greatest obligation is to humanity itself. We have to reach up to the Source of life itself as we have done earlier, and continue energizing the principles of peace, prosperity, and progress. You can add to this the vision of all-encompassing love for all people. Love for the enemy as well as the neighbor. Love for the God of all, not the God of the few.

With your growing psychic powers and skills, use them to see beyond partisanship and separatism, and use them to reach out and turn off the teaching of hate and divisiveness, of repression and imposed ignorance, and the subjugation of personal morality. Replace them with the three E's of enlightenment, enrichment, and empowerment—**EEE**.

Then we will have earned a future of renewal and a true New Age, established in higher consciousness and expanded awareness. In a New Order for the Ages—Novus Ordo Seclorum.

References

Lynne McTaggart, *The Intention Experiment* (New York: Free Press, 2007).

Roget's II: The New Thesaurus (Houghton Mifflin, Boston, 1995).

CHAPTER ELEVEN

THE PSYCHIC EMPOWERMENT PLAN
Personal Responsibility for Continued Growth and Development

IT'S YOUR JOB NOW!

While the psychic empowerment plan is presented as a seven-day program, *it— along with all the various exercises and programs presented throughout the book—can and should be adapted to your continuing individual development program.* It is important to accept the personal responsibility to continue the growing and developing of your greater self and the skills to use the powers you have in everyday life.

Don't just settle back into complacency, knowing that you do have psychic powers that will occasionally manifest and help you. Take up the challenge to become more than you are! Take up the challenge to transform your life! Take up the challenge of helping to change the world for the better! Take up the challenge to consciously communicate with your own subconscious mind and through it with the collective unconscious! Take up the challenge to communicate with your own inner guide, your higher self, and spiritual entities! And take up the challenge of living your life as the great adventure and fulfilling your part in the great plan that is fundamental to our very existence!

Your psychic empowerment is the most important responsibility you have as an adult human being, for it gives you the powers to better fulfill all your other responsibilities to self, family, and society.

In all these programs and exercises, see the importance of your imagination—not as a passive source of pleasure or fear, but as a positive resource opening doors to the subconscious mind and expanding your awareness to the whole person you are.

Clearly, psychic empowerment is for everyone. Now as never before, you can develop your psychic potentials to enrich your life with new growth and power. Your past is a vast body of resources, and your future is a vast body of possibilities. The present is yours at the moment. You can embrace it right now to empower your life. Once fully empowered, nothing is beyond your reach. You can shape your own future and write your own destiny. You can set your highest goals and achieve them while bringing forth needed change in the world. You can do it all, and you can begin right now.

We now know that psychic empowerment, rather than a product, is a never-ending process of growth and self-discovery. It's a process that's at your full command. You can focus it inwardly to activate your existing potentials and create new ones. You can focus it outwardly to access totally new sources of power. The seven-day psychic empowerment plan that follows is designed to do both. Through this plan, you can take charge of your present life and your future alike.

This is a powerful but flexible plan—it is not written in stone. You can easily adapt it to fit your own interests and personal needs. To maximize its effectiveness, however, repeated practice is essential. As you progress from day to day, take the previous programs along with you and use them as needed. Give special attention to daily programs that hold special relevance for you, and don't hesitate to use them as needed. With practice, they will increase in relevance and power.

Once you have completed this seven-day program, adapt it to continue on, week-after-week, with a continued program for constant growth and success. The first week is just a start, for you now have the foundation of your own life-long program.

Psychic empowerment is your start toward true Self Empowerment.

A SEVEN-DAY JOURNEY FOR SPIRITUAL GROWTH, SELF-DISCOVERY, AND SUCCESS

The seven-day journey that follows charts a new direction for your spiritual growth, self-discovery, and success. Once you've started, let nothing interrupt the journey. *Bon voyage!*

Day One: Attunement and Balance Interaction

The first day of the psychic empowerment plan lays the foundation for the remaining six days. It recognizes the spirit realm from which we all came and to which we will all return as an ever-present dimension that invites our contact and interaction. As evolving spiritual beings, we can become balanced and attuned to that realm with its abundance of growth energy. Attunement and balance are interactive states of mind, body, and spirit in which the frequencies of your own energies come into harmony with those of higher spiritual planes. Once balanced within and attuned to the spirit realm, you will become empowered with an abundance of new growth energy that will enrich the quality of your life. The program that follows is designed to achieve that important goal.

1. **Centering.** While resting comfortably, close your eyes and clear your mind by centering your thoughts on your breathing. Feel the fresh air soaking into your lungs as you breathe slowly and deeply, taking plenty of time to develop a comfortable, rhythmic breathing pattern.

2. **Imaging.** As you remain in that comfortable state, allow peaceful images to flow gently in and out of your mind. Notice the color, motion, and details of the images as they come and go spontaneously.

3. **Focusing.** From among the images flowing through your mind, select one that seems right for you at the moment and focus your full attention on it. Flow with that image and let yourself become a part of it. Become so absorbed with the image that you seem to lose yourself in the experience. Stay with the image as you sense yourself absorbing its positive energies.

4. **Serenity.** Let the image finally dissolve away, leaving behind a serene state of wellbeing. Your mind is now emptied of all active thought. The energies of your being are now positive, synchronized, and balanced.

5. **Bright Energy.** Sense the bright energy of a higher source slowly enveloping your body and infusing your own energy system. Sense the energies of your being interacting with the bright energies from beyond. Let yourself become fully infused and attuned to that merging of energies.

6. **Affirmation.** Affirm in your own words the powerful attuning and balancing effects of this program.

7. **Empowerment.** Conclude with the affirmation that you can at any time or place activate in an instant the full empowering effect of this program by simply visualizing bright energy of a higher source enveloping your full body.

Like the other programs in this plan, practice improves the effectiveness of this procedure. Daily practice of this program is recommended for the duration of the seven-day plan.

Day Two: A Leaf in Hand

The program for day two of our plan is designed to unleash a powerful flow of new growth energy by tapping into the highest sources of power. It's based on the premise that your hands are your body's antennae and the tree is the earth's antennae. When you link the two, you become infused with energy in its purest and most powerful form. Here's the program called A Leaf in Hand.

1. **Selection.** Select a leaf from a tree of your choice, preferably a tree that has special appeal to you. Remove the leaf, being careful not to tear it. (Note: if a real leaf is not available to you because of season or location, you can use visualization of a leaf and a tree as an effective representation.)

2. **Connection.** Find a comfortable place, settle back, and place the leaf between your palms.

3. **Sensation.** With the leaf resting between your palms, close your eyes and visualize the leaf as you sense its energies. Notice the pleasurable sensation of simply having a leaf resting in your hands. Think of your hands as your body's antennae and the leaf as your connection to the tree as earth's antenna to the universe.

4. **Visualization.** As the leaf continues to rest between your palms, visualize the tree from which it was taken. Notice the tree's size and unique characteristics, keeping in mind that trees, like people, are unique, with no two being exactly alike.

5. **Energy Infusion.** With the leaf in your hands, sense your connection to the tree and the powerful infusion of energy flowing first into your hands, and then throughout your body.

6. **Empowerment.** Take plenty of time for the infusion of new energy to reach its peak. In that empowered state, you can bring fulfillment, happiness, and success into your life. You are now empowered to achieve your personal goals, whether mental, physical, or spiritual. You now have access to the highest sources of enlightenment and power. It's not an exaggeration to affirm: "Greatness is my destiny."

7. **Reactivation.** Before returning the leaf to the earth, tell yourself in your own words that you can at any moment reactivate the empowering effects of this experience by simply bringing your palms together as you visualize the leaf resting between them.

A Leaf in Hand is one of the best programs known for psychic development. It not only activates a variety of psychic functions, it stimulates their continued development. The result is an empowered state with wide-ranging possibilities—expanding awareness, reducing stress, breaking unwanted habits, slowing aging, and promoting wellness, to list only a few. *You will find the effectiveness of this exercise increases with repeated practice.*

Day Three: The Aura Massage

The aura is an external manifestation of the internal energy force that sustains your existence as a soul being. As an energy phenomenon, it envelops your full body, and under certain circumstances, it becomes clearly visible. Your personal aura is your unique spiritual signature that represents your spiritual makeup as an evolving soul. Consequently, no two auras are exactly alike. While basically stable in color and structure, the aura is influenced by both internal and external conditions. It can, for instance, become discolored by a depressed mood state and constricted by excessive stress. It can become imbalanced by conflict and insecurity. Fortunately, it is always receptive to your intervention. You can balance, attune, energize, and fully empower it. The aura massage as presented here is designed to achieve that important goal.

1. **Viewing the Aura.** With your hand held at arm's length against a neutral background, spread your fingers and focus your full attention on your middle finger. Slowly expand your peripheral vision to take in the full background—above, below, and to each side of your hand. Once your peripheral vision reaches its outer limits, let your eyes fall slightly out of focus and you will note a colorless glow around your hand, a forerunner to the appearance of the aura. Continue to view your hand with its surrounding glow until the aura with its color and structure comes into view. Take a few moments to view the aura around your hand, paying particular attention to its expansiveness and intensity. Remind yourself that the aura around your hand is representative of the aura enveloping your full body. (Note: Viewing your aura may require more than one practice session.)

2. **Central Body Aura Massage.** Having viewed the aura, you are now ready to begin the aura massage, using your hands held at a few inches from your body. Carefully avoiding any physical contact with the body, begin the massage with slow, circular hand movements around your central body or solar plexus region. Start with small circular movements and then gradu-

ally expand them to take in the lower and upper body regions. You can sense during the massage its internal energizing effects, not only in your central body, but throughout your full body as well.

3. **Head Region Aura Massage.** Upon completing the central body massage, shift the massage to your head region. Begin by closing your eyes and bringing your hands to each side of your head, careful as before to avoid physical touch. Begin with your hands held to each side of your head and start the massage with very slow, small circular hand movements. Expand the circular movements as you sense the comforting, peaceful effects deep within. Notice the clearing of clutter from your mind as the infusion of bright energy spreads throughout your total being.

4. **Aura Post-Viewing.** Again view your aura as in Step 1. Notice specifically the expansiveness of the aura, along with the increased brightness of its colors.

5. **Affirmation.** Conclude the massage with affirmations of its energizing, balancing, and attuning effects.

Through practice, the aura massage becomes increasingly effective. It can be used while standing, sitting, clothed, or unclothed. You can use it before falling asleep or as preparation for an important conference or presentation. It can be used even while showering. *Repeat often—especially when anything occurs to remind you of the powerful effects of Aura Massage you've just experienced.*

Day Four: Pyramid of Power

Visualization and positive affirmation together form the holy grail of psychic empowerment. Nothing is more powerful mentally, physically, or spiritually. If a picture is worth a thousand words, it increases a thousand fold when combined with self-affirmation. Day four of our plan integrates the power of images and words in a step-by-step program that generates a progressive synergistic effect with absolutely no limits. You can take it as far as you wish to go. Called Pyramid of

Power, this program, once set into motion, initiates a timeless progression of growth with unlimited possibilities. Here's the program.

1. **Connection.** Settle back into a comfortable seated or reclining position, and with your eyes closed, slow your breathing as you clear your mind of all active thought. As you become increasingly relaxed, visualize a glowing pyramid with steps leading to its apex. Further visualize a radiant beam of light connecting you to the pyramid and infusing you with the pyramid's powerful energy. Take plenty of time for the infusion process to run its course.

2. **Ascension.** Beginning at the pyramid's base, mentally ascend the pyramid step by step, pausing long enough along the way to form affirmations related to your present life goals and strivings. Think of the pyramid's steps as symbols of your progress. Think of your affirmations as confirmations of that progress and your future success. The steps and affirmations can relate to personal goals, problem situations, relationships, or any other concern of relevance to your life at the moment. As you ascend the pyramid step by step, accompany the affirmations with visualization of yourself enveloped in the glowing energies of the pyramid.

3. **Infusion.** Upon reaching the pyramid's apex, sense your connection to the highest realms of power and let yourself become infused with bright energy. Think of the pyramid as your personal link to mental, physical, and spiritual power. Allow plenty of time for the infusion of powerful energy to reach its peak.

4. **Affirmation.** Conclude the program by affirming in your own words the empowering effects of the experience. Further affirm that by simply visualizing the pyramid enveloped in bright energy, you can at any moment activate the full empowering effects of this program.

Add the Pyramid of Power to your repertoire of psychic empowerment skills and use it whenever needed. *With practice, it will become your personal link to power in its purest form.*

Day Five: The Blank Screen

Your ability to clear your mind and center your thoughts is essential to psychic empowerment. In that cleared and centered state, your psychic powers are at their peak and your psychic development is accelerated. The blank screen is designed to generate that state. When practiced regularly, this simple exercise can enrich your life and promote your continuous psychic growth. *It can activate in an instant your psychic faculties and generate the power required to achieve your personal goals.* Here's the program, which requires around thirty minutes.

1. **Relax and Focus.** In a quiet, comfortable place free of distractions, settle back and take in a few deep breaths, exhaling slowly. Close your eyes and focus your full attention on your breathing as you develop a slow, rhythmic breathing pattern.

2. **Relax and Scan.** Beginning at your forehead, scan your body from your forehead downward, pausing at stress points and letting the tension go. Let your body become fully relaxed as you continue to breathe slowly and rhythmically.

3. **Visualize the Blank Screen.** As your eyes remain closed and your body fully relaxed, visualize a blank screen against a dark background. Focus your full attention on the screen and allow a triangle to form upon it. Think of the triangle's three points as the three essential components of your being: mind, body, and spirit. Think of the interior of the triangle as the merging of those components. Notice the emergent glow, first within the triangle and then surrounding it. As the glow slowly expands, sense the infusion of powerful energy throughout your total being.

4. **Form the Triangle.** Once the energy surge reaches its peak, form a triangle with your hands by joining the tips of your thumbs to form its base, and the tips of your index fingers to

form its apex. You will instantly experience a serene state of balance and attunement.

5. **Personal Goals.** While continuing to hold the triangle, shift your attention to your personal goals, including the development of your psychic potentials, and affirm your power to achieve them.

6. **Affirmation.** Conclude this program by relaxing your hands and affirming in your own words that by simply forming a triangle with your hands, you can activate at any time the full effects of this program.

This exercise has wide-ranging applications and can be used for almost any personal goal. It is especially effective when used as a clairvoyant and precognitive strategy. Not infrequently, images of future relevance will appear on the screen. It can also be used to activate your creative faculties. It has been used by musicians and artists alike to generate creative materials. Aside from these applications, the program is highly effective in breaking unwanted habits, such as quitting smoking or managing weight. You can use the hand triangle as a cue at any time to build the determination needed for your total success.

Day Six: The Orb of Power

You are an energy being, but you are far more than that. You are a unique life-force entity with power to both send and receive energy. *Through this program called the Orb of Power, you have direct access to the energy sources, both within yourself and beyond.* Given abundant energy, you become empowered to focus and disperse it as needed to achieve even your most difficult goals. You can even disperse energy on a global scale to make the world a better place.

1. **Attunement.** Immediately upon awakening from sleep and before beginning the day, take a few minutes simply to reflect on the moment and let yourself become attuned to it. Turn your thoughts inward as you sense the wonder of your existence.

2. **Energy Interaction.** Sense bright energy flowing within your being and let yourself become fully attuned to it. Let the bright energy within radiate beyond yourself to interact with higher planes of energy. Visualize the energy interaction as it unfolds while sensing its energizing effects.

3. **Orb Visualization.** As you continue to sense interacting energies flowing within your being, bring your hands together and take a few moments to rub them briskly against each other. Sense the warm, tingling energy building between your hands. After a few moments of palm-against-palm motion, separate your hands and visualize an orb of energy forming between then. Given dim natural lighting, you may, in fact, actually see the orb glowing brightly between your hands.

4. **Set the Goal.** With the orb of energy glowing between your hands, affirm your power to disperse it. At this point, you may wish to specify a goal, or you may wish to send forth bright energy as a positive force that's dispersed without limits.

5. **Sending Forth.** To disperse the energy, simply relax your hands and allow the orb of energy to go forth.

This program recognizes the interactive nature of psychic empowerment. Exercising your psychic skills empowers you mentally, physically, and spiritually. *Through this program, you can access energy and focus it in ways that enrich your life and ensure your complete success, regardless of the nature of your goals.*

Day 7: The Greater Good

Psychic empowerment is a dynamic process of growth and self-discovery. It recognizes the incomparable worth of all human beings and our capacity for growth and change. Aside from its direct and immediate empowering effects, it's a goal-oriented phenomenon that can awaken your dormant potentials and focus them as needed to enrich your life.

At its peak, psychic empowerment transcends the self and centers on the needs of others. World needs and global concerns are not beyond the scope of psychic empowerment. It's a growth- and action-related phenomenon that seeks solutions to such issues as world hunger, poverty, injustice, abuse of human and animal rights, disease, discrimination, pollution, and reckless exploitation of our natural resources.

Day seven of our plan is built on the premise that the simplest program is often the most effective. Rather than a step-by-step procedure, it consists simply of intention and interaction for the greater good. While not prescribing specific goals, it recognizes the value of simply performing a daily act of kindness toward people and animals alike. It recognizes the value of sending forth a positive thought message of caring and hope. On a larger scale, it recognizes the importance of such worthy causes as nurturing the planet, alleviating world hunger, and promoting peace. It accepts the principle that if every person on the planet sent forth at least one positive thought message, and performed at least one act of kindness every day, the effects would resonate around the world. The earth would then become a better place and life upon it would be enriched.

COMMITMENT, ENERGY, AND ACTION

When the dots are finally connected and the line is drawn, the major goal of psychic empowerment is twofold: *actualizing your highest potentials while—equally as important— using them for the greater good.* It's an essential goal for which there is no substitute. Psychic empowerment can equip you with the three things needed to reach that goal: commitment, energy, and action. Given these essentials, nothing is beyond your reach.

With psychic empowerment, you open your potential for self-empowerment through development and training of your psychic powers into reliable psychic skills that enlighten your whole person.

SPECIALIZED GLOSSARY OF PSYCHIC TERMINOLOGY AND SUGGESTED READING

It is important to understand that a glossary is neither a dictionary nor an encyclopedia. Most of the definitions given here are specific to the words as used in this book, although we have included others of interest to psychic and paranormal study. In some cases, readings are suggested for further research on the subject involved. We have also included some short definitions of paranormal phenomena that may or may not have a psychic connection but are often accompanied by increased psychic sensibilities.

The intention of this glossary is to give you more in order to provide more growth opportunities. Once you start *becoming more than you are,* keep on going, and going, and going. Let these definitions call out to you, and listen to your subconscious give particular clues for your own developmental program.

Ajna. The brow chakra.

Akashic Records. The enduring records of everything that has ever happened, the repository of all knowledge and wisdom, and the files of every personal memory. It is believed to exist on the higher astral and lower mental planes and to be accessible by the super consciousness through the subconscious mind in deep-trance states induced through hypnosis, self-hypnosis, meditation, and guided meditation.

Aliens. Generally associated with UFOs, semi-humanoid beings claiming to originate on other planets or other dimensions. Most contacts with these beings involve telepathic communication and some have included abductions and transportation to space ships where surgical operations have implanted devices, and others have included sexual contact. Some believe aliens are spirits and that alien encounters are psychic in nature, and others suggest that they are particular expressions of the subconsciousness.

Suggested Reading: Jang, *The Gaia Project, 2012 the Earth's Coming Great Changes.*

Suggested Reading: Imbrogno, *Interdimensional Universe: The New Science of UFOs, Paranormal Phenomena & Other Dimensional Beings.*

Alpha Level. The brain generates weak electrical impulses representative of its particular activities. As recorded by the electroencephalograph (EEG), they fall into particular levels assigned Greek letters. Beta, at 14 to 26 cycles per second, is our normal waking state including focused attention, concentration, thinking, etc. Alpha, 8 to 13 cycles, is the next level down, characteristic of relaxation, alert receptivity, meditation and access to the subconscious mind. It is at 8 cycles per second, the border between alpha and theta that trance occurs. Theta, 4 to 7, is lower yet and occurs just before hypnopompic or after hypnagogic sleep and is characteristic of light sleep, deep meditation, vivid imagery, and high levels of inner awareness. Delta, 0.5 to 3, is characteristic of deep sleep—but has also been recorded in connection with deep meditation.

Altered State of Consciousness (ASC). Wakefulness and sleep are the two most familiar states of consciousness. Others include dreaming, meditation, trance, hypnosis and self-hypnosis, hallucination, astral projection, etc. ASCs can be induced by sleep deprivation, chanting, fasting, ecstatic dancing, drumming, sex, psychedelic drugs, and conscious self-programming. Once you've been there, it is easier to get there again.

Anahata. The heart chakra.

Apparition. A projection of one's image that is seen by another. Unlike astral projection, the appearance is mostly spontaneous and does not involve the projector entering into a trance state. Apparitions are often connected with a personal crisis or intense interest in the other person. Sometimes the apparition is coincidental with the person's death.

Apport. The appearance of an object as if moved from another location by psychic means. It is believed to involve the de-materialization and then re-materialization of the object.

Armageddon. As described in the Christian Bible, the final battle between good and evil marking the end of the world. It is a mythical reality, an image that challenges us to resolve. It is not historically inevitable, but rather a call to action.

Astral Body. The third body or level of consciousness, and is also called the emotional body and the subtle body. It encompasses the field of dreams, the imagination, and the subconscious mind. It is the vehicle for most psychic activities.

Astral Doorways. Particular symbols and images, including Tarot cards, Tattwas, and Yantras used in meditation to gain access to specific parts of the astral plane and to corresponding subjective states of consciousness.

Suggested Reading: Tyson, *Soul Flight: Astral Projection & the Magical Universe.*

Astral Light. It is approximately equivalent to ether, mana, and vital fluid, and is the substance of the astral plane which holds the impressions of thought and emotion.

Astral Plane. The second plane, sometimes called the inner plane or subjective world, it is an alternate dimension both coincidental to our physical world and extending beyond it. Some believe it extends to other planets and allows for astral travel between them.

Astral Projection. A particular state of consciousness in which the astral body separates from the physical and is able to travel on the astral plane, obtain information, communicate with other beings, and return to the physical with full memory. While it is commonly thought that the astral body separates from the physical during sleep, other investigators consider it an extension of consciousness that does not travel. Sometimes, the astral body sees the physical world and can report on physical incidents.

Suggested Reading: Bruce & Mercer, *Mastering Astral Projection.*

Suggested Reading: Denning and Phillips, *Practical Guide to Astral Projection, The Out-of-Body Experience.*

Astral Travel. Astral projection specifically involving travel to defined locations—sometimes as observation of physical places and others of astral places.

Suggested Reading: Goldberg, *Astral Voyages, Mastering the Art of Interdimensional Travel.*

Suggested Reading: Webster, *Astral Travel for Beginners: Transcend Time & Space with Out-of-Body Experiences.*

Astrology. *Astronomy brought down to earth.* This is the science that relates planetary patterns measured by positions in the sky, and mapped in relation to the physical location and time of birth of a person or an event, to a very long tradition of observation and interpretation in order to describe the character of the person or event.

Suggested Reading: George, *Llewellyn's New A to Z Horoscope Maker & Interpreter: A Comprehensive Self-study Course.*

Suggested Reading: Riske, *Llewellyn's Complete Book of Astrology: the Easy Way to Learn Astrology.*

Atman. The higher self or soul that is eternal.

Aura. A field of energy surrounding the physical body and viewed by clairvoyants in colorful layers that may be read and interpreted.

Suggested Reading: Slate, *Aura Energy for Health, Healing & Balance.*

Aura Reading. Clairvoyant reading of the aura to determine the health, character, and spiritual development of the person (or animal) by the colors seen.

Suggested Reading: Andrews, *How to See and Read the Aura.*

Suggested Reading: Webster, *Aura Reading for Beginners: Develop Your Psychic Awareness for Health & Success.*

Automatic Writing. A form of channeling in which a person, sometimes in trance, writes or even keyboards messages generally believed to originate with spiritual beings, or with aspects of the subconscious mind.

Awareness. Conscious perception from which memory is derived.

"Bad Vibes." An uncomfortable sensation experienced in connection with person or place and interpreted as a forewarning of something dire. It may be considered as a message from the subconscious.

Belief System. The complex of feelings that defines the way we perceive reality. Also see Feelings and Operating System. Belief is also described as faith that filters our perception of reality as defined by religious and cultural institutions. Because it has been formed through unconscious conditioning, we need to consciously analyze it for its valid pertinence in our lives.

Suggested Reading: Bradden, *The Spontaneous Healing of Belief, Shattering the Paradigm of False Limits.*

Bi-Directional Endlessness. From the reincarnation perspective, the continuum for individual existence is endless, with neither beginning nor end.

Bi-Location. Instances where a person appears simultaneously in two separate locations, one of which is believed to be the physical body and the other the astral body.

Biofeedback. The use of instrumentation to measure the effects of various mental processes including imagery and suggestion on such biological functions as brainwave patterns, finger temperature, and galvanic skin response. It provides a mechanism to explore past conditioning in terms of a healthy lifestyle.

Brainstorming. Commonly a group search for new ideas, or for new applications for old ideas. It's best done as a rapid-fire, free-for-all, idea jam-session opening the psychic faculties to inspiration. See Inspiration.

Buddic Plane. The fourth plane up from the physical, sometimes called the intuitional level.

Chakras. Whirling centers of energy associated with particular areas of the body. In the Hindu tradition, *muladhara* is located at the base of the spine and is the source of *kundalini* and the power used in sex magic. *Svadhisthna* is located at the sacrum. *Muladhara* and *svadhisthna* are linked to the physical body. *Manipura* is located at the solar plexus. *Muladhara, svadhisthna,* and *manipura* are together associated as the personality, and their energies can be projected through the solar plexus in such psychic phenomena as rapping, ectoplasm, and the creation of familiars.

   Manipura is linked to the lower astral body. *Anahata* is located at the heart and is associated with group consciousness. *Vishuddha* is located at the throat and is associated with clairvoyance. *Anahata* and *Ajna* are linked to the higher astral body. *Ajna* is located at the brow and is associated with clairvoyance. *Sahasrara* is located at the crown and is associated with spiritual consciousness. *Anahata, vishuddha,* and *sahasrara* are together associated as the spiritual self.

   Suggested Reading: Judith, *Wheels of Life: A User's Guide to the Chakra System.*

   Suggested Reading: Mumford, *Chakra & Kundalini Workbook: Psycho-spiritual Techniques for Health, Rejuvenation, Psychic Powers & Spiritual Rejuvenation.*

Channels. (1) An alternate name for a medium, and (2) a specific connection similar to a television channel for astral and mental plane communications.

Channeling. Receiving information from a discarnate entity or a higher spiritual being. It may also refer to communication with an aspect of one's own subconscious mind.

Chanting. The repetition of words or short phrases in a vibrating voice that stirs psychic energy and may induce trance.

   Suggested Reading: Andrews, *Sacred Sounds, Magic & Healing through Words & Music.*

Chi. The Chinese name for vital energy comparable to the Hindu *Prana*.

Suggested Reading: Shaw, *Chi Kung for Beginners: Master the Flow of Chi for Good Health, Stress Reduction & Increased Energy*.

Circle. A temporary boundary within which a séance or magical operation may take place. The theory is that it becomes a kind of psychic container for the energies used in the operation and a barrier to unwanted energies from outside.

Clairaudience. Extrasensory perception (ESP) experienced in astral hearing.

Clairvoyance. ESP experience in etheric and astral seeing. Some clairvoyants can also perceive on the mental plane.

Suggested Reading: Katz, *You Are Psychic: The Art of Clairvoyant Reading & Healing*.

Suggested Reading: Owens, *Spiritualism & Clairvoyance for Beginners: Simple Techniques to Develop Your Psychic Abilities*.

Close Encounters. In UFO lore, contact between human and alien beings. There is much to suggest that these may not be physical beings but perhaps projections of the unconscious. There are paranormal, psychic, and psychological factors to be considered.

Cognitive Relaxation. Inducing physical relaxation through intervention into the mental functions related to relaxation. Common examples are the use of visualization and suggestion to induce a peaceful, relaxed state.

Coincidence. A seeming simultaneous happening, the meaning of which may be personal.

Collective Unconscious. A kind of group consciousness inclusive of shared memories and the collective knowledge of all humanity that may be centered in our genetic code. It is the home of archetypes, those apparent entities that represent our collective experience of such universal beings as the Wise Woman, the Hero, the Great Mother, the Benevolent Leader, the Magician, etc. as seen on the Tarot cards, in universal myths, and religious icons. The archetypes may be the gods, each charged with particular responsibilities in the natural world. See also Noosphere.

Consciousness. The beginning of all things and part of the trinity of consciousness, energy, and matter. It includes all states of awareness and our experience of fear, love, hope, desire, happiness, sadness, depression, ecstasy, mystical union, etc. We experience connectedness through consciousness.

Control. The spirit who acts as a kind of manager through which other spirits communicate with the medium during a seance.

Cosmic Consciousness. A phrase coined by Richard Bucke to describe his own experience of unity with the universal consciousness of the cosmos. Bucke believed this to be the goal of human evolution.

Suggested Reading: Bucke, *Cosmic Consciousness*.

Crop Circles. Sometimes associated with, but not limited to, UFO lore in which (1) often crudely formed amateur geometric patterns are found in agricultural fields of such crops as grass, corn, wheat, etc., (2) finely detailed and professional complex geometric patterns in the midst of field crops. In both instances, these large-scale drawings happen at night. In most of the amateur class examples, pranksters have admitted to dragging wood beams to break down the crops. In cases of the professional class examples, no *human* explanations have been uncovered. Theories range from alien communications to unusual natural gravitational or electromagnetic effects. Until understood, the phenomenon remains classed as paranormal.

Crystal Ball. A round ball of quartz crystal or glass used as focal point in scrying. Gazing at the ball, one enters into a trance-like state where dream-like scenes and symbols are seen and interpreted. Similar fascination aids are the magic mirror, a pool of black ink, a piece of obsidian, even a bottle of water.

Suggested Reading: Andrews, *Crystal Balls & Crystal Bowls, Tools for Ancient Scrying & Modern Seership*.

Suggested Reading: Cunningham, *Divination for Beginners: Reading the Past, Present & Future*.

Direct Voice. When a medium allows a spirit to directly speak through her/him, it appears to be the voice of the deceased and sometimes so strongly contrasts with the medium's normal voice as to seem impossible.

Dowsing. Psychic empathy with the natural world enabling the practitioner to locate water, ores, petroleum, ley lines, etc., usually aided by a device such as a forked stick, pendulum, or a modified set of coat hangers which will strongly respond in the dowser's hands when he or she is walking over the physical location. Some dowsers work with a pendulum and a large-scale map, and obtain equally valid results.

Suggested Reading: Webster, *Dowsing for Beginners: How to Find Water, Wealth & Lost Objects.*

Dreaming True. Programmed dreaming where a question or an intention is formulated before sleep, and left to the subconscious mind to respond with an answer or an action. It usually involves a study of the possibilities before sleep.

Dreams. Stories experienced during sleep. Sometimes dreams seem merely to be translations of physical experiences, others seem to be ways we assimilate new information. Dreams are also a function of the subconscious mind and deliberate dreaming is a doorway into the subconscious and its connection to the collective unconscious.

Suggested Reading: Gongloff, *Dream Exploration: A New Approach.*

Suggested Reading: González-Wippler, *Dreams & What They Mean to You.*

Earthbound Spirits. The belief that some spirits, especially those dying in sudden and unexpected transitions, or the spirits of children, cling to the earth experience they knew, fear moving on, and resist the natural process.

Suggested Reading: Crawford, *Spirit of Love: A Medium's Message of Life Beyond Death.*

Suggested Reading: Davidson, *Spirit Rescue: A Simple Guide to Talking with Ghosts and Freeing Earthbound Souls.*

Ectoplasm. A mist-like substance emitted from various body orifices of the medium, believed to originate from the etheric body.

Elan Vital. Vital energy, Prana, Chi.

Electrophotography. Developed by the Russian scientists Semyon and Valentina Kirlian in 1939, electrophotography is a contact technique in which the object being photographed, such as a finger tip, is placed in direct contact with film placed on a metal plate charged with electricity of high voltage and frequency. Electrophotography was hailed by many parapsychologists as "a way to see the unseeable" and "a window on the unknown, which could revolutionize our concept of self and the universe." Ostrander and Schroeder concluded that the Kirlians had photographed the etheric or energy body and provided a new technique for "exploring the energy body of ESP."

Suggested Reading: Ostrander, Schroeder, and Sanderson, *Psychic Discoveries Behind the Iron Curtain.*

Elemental. (1) Nonhuman nature spirits associated with different natural elements of Earth, Water, Air, and Fire. (2) A thought form charged with energy and intention by a magician to carry out a particular operation, such as a household guardian.

Emotion. "Energy in motion." Emotion is a dynamic and powerful response to something perceived that connects to universal human experience and archetypes. Emotion is the energy powering most intentional psychic and magical operations, the energy responsible for many types of psychic phenomena, possibly including hauntings, poltergeists, rapping, etc. where there is potential for the emotion to have been recorded in the woodwork of the building.

Ether. Identical with the Hindu *Akasha* and the fifth element in Western magic, spirit, which is believed to originate the other four: Earth, Water, Fire, and Air. See also Astral Light, Odic Force, Orgone, the Force.

Etheric Body. The second body, or energy body, which is fully coincident with the physical body in health.

Etheric Plane. Basically the higher, energy part of the physical plane.

Expectancy Effect. The effect of expectation on the future, to include personal performance and outcomes, with expectations of success typically facilitating success.

Extrasensory Perception (ESP). The awareness of or response to events, conditions, and situations independently of known sensory mechanisms or processes.

Feelings. An instinctive response conveying some truth about a person or situation. It is a kind of filter through which we experience reality. Also see Operating System.

Field. The first thing, the field of manifestation, consciousness, from which first energy and then matter arose as energy/matter packets that manifest as waves or particles. The field is the source for all that follows—today as yesterday and as tomorrow. The field can be accessed through deliberate thought and responds to emotion expressed with intention. Through the field we can change reality, hence it is the field of magic, phenomena, and of miraculous things that matter.

Suggested Reading: McTaggart, *The Field: The Quest for the Secret Force of the Universe.*

Suggested Reading: McTaggart, *The Intention Experiment, Using Your Thoughts to Change Your Life and the World.*

Force, the. The primal energy in the field. As the force, prana, chi, orgone, etc. it is everywhere and is the power the gives us life.

Ghosts. (1) Earthbound spirits haunting a particular location. (2) A psychic recording of emotional energy released during traumatic experiences of suicide, murder, accidental death and painful dying. As a psychic recording, it can be reproduced and experienced by psychically sensitive people and almost always at night when nothing competes with the reception. These experiences are often accompanied by fear, which then reinforces the initial energy. Like other kinds of recording, the original energy can often be released or erased by overwriting with other strong releases of emotion such as a ritual exorcism, happy children, shamanic practices, and even loud music.

Suggested Reading: Danelek, *The Case for Ghosts: An Objective Look at the Paranormal.*

Suggested Reading: Wilder, *House of Spirits and Whispers: The True Story of a Haunted House.*

Great Plan, the. Some occultists believe that there is a plan guiding the evolution of human consciousness to its eventual reunion with the ultimate Source.

Suggested Reading: almost any book by Alice Bailey.

Guided Imagery. The use of suggestion and visualization to guide thought processes, typically to promote a positive state of physical relaxation and personal well-being. Guided imagery can, however, be used to induce a trance state or as a goal-oriented technique for managing stress or pain, overcoming fear, breaking unwanted habits, slowing aging, and promoting wellness, to mention but a few of the possibilities.

Guided Meditation. A meditation led by an experienced guide following established inner pathways to access particular iconic collections of knowledge and experience. A typical example would be found in Kabbalistic pathworkings progressing on the path from one sphere to another on the Tree of Life.

Suggested Reading: Clayton, *Transformative Meditation: Personal & Group Practice to Access Realms of Consciousness.*

Lorenzo-Fuentes, *Meditation.*

Regardie, with the Ciceros, *A Garden of Pomegranates, Skrying on the Tree of Life.*

Hauntings. See Ghosts. Hauntings are confined to specific physical spaces and are associated with such experiences as bad vibes and uncomfortable feelings, strange and scary sounds, sights of swirling mists, and of deceased people. The phenomenon almost always occurs at night when there is no competition for the experience and most often in locations that are rarely disturbed, such as abandoned houses and churches, old cemeteries, ancient religious sites, etc. There are claims that haunting experiences fluctuate with the phases of the Moon.

Suggested Reading: Belanger, *Haunting Experiences: Encounters with the Otherworldly.*

Suggested Reading: Goodwyn, *Ghost Worlds, A Guide to Poltergeists, Portals, Ecto-mist & Spirit Behavior.*

Holism. The whole view. Seeing things from a fully organic perspective inclusive of all the levels of life, consciousness, and manifestation. It's all the connections seen at once. This is an *essential* perspective fostering your balanced psychic development and empowerment.

Horoscope. A map of the planetary positions at any moment in time as seen from perception a point on the earth's surface. It is the form from which astrological interpretations are given based upon thousands of years of observed coincidental phenomena.

Suggested Reading: Clement, *Mapping Your Birthchart: Understanding Your Needs & Potential.*

Suggested Reading: Perry, Wendell. *Saturn Cycles, Mapping Changes in Your Life.*

Hunch. Intuition. A feeling expressing the truth of a situation.

Hypnogenerativity. Self-hypnosis brings together a host of subconscious processes in ways that generate totally new resources and growth possibilities that are often inclusive of psychic skills.

Hypnoproduction. New abilities that may develop through self-hypnosis, including instantaneous command of a new language and sudden mastery of an artistic or scientific skill, each of which could be explained as the retrieval of skills acquired in a past life including those of a psychic nature.

Hypnosis (see also Self-Hypnosis). An altered state of consciousness that provides a bridge to the subconscious mind by which conscious commands mobilize subconscious resources including current and past-life memories, and exercise certain control over physical body responses to external stimuli and internal functions, access areas of the collective unconscious, and channels communication between astral and mental levels and the physical level. The hypnotic trance has been associated with various psychic abilities.

Suggested Reading: Hewitt, *Hypnosis for Beginners: Reach New Levels of Awareness & Achievement.*

I AM. The identifying phrase in a powerful self-affirmation used in self-hypnosis.

I Ching. A Chinese divinatory system of sixty-four hexagrams that express the dynamic flow of energies into their physical manifestation. Like most divination, it is a manipulative system calling forth the practitioner's psychic abilities.

Suggested Reading: Brennan, *The Magical I Ching.*

Suggested Reading: McElroy, *I Ching for Beginners: A Modern Interpretation of the Ancient Oracle.*

Information. Programs of instruction and memories that control the transfers of energy and matter.

Information Packets. Combinations of programs controlling a numbers of processes. In the body they instruct how each tiny cell functions, how every organ does its work, how every nerve and every vein carries energies and hormones to designated places, and how everything relates together to make a functioning and healthy body.

Inspiration. Usually a sequence of ideas suggesting particular actions, originating at the psychic level. It is often associated with brainstorming, and is especially productive in a group setting. See Brainstorming.

Suggested Reading: McElroy, *The Bright Idea Deck.*

Suggested Reading: McElroy, *Putting the Tarot to Work.*

Intuition. A blinding flash of insight answering a question or solving a problem originating at the Soul level of consciousness.

Kabbalah. A complete system of knowledge about all the dimensions of the universe and of the human psyche organized into the Tree of Life diagram showing the inner construction and the connections between levels and forms of consciousness, energy, and matter. It provides a resource for understanding and applying the principles of magick, for understanding the dynamics of the psyche, and for interpreting human history and action. The present-day Tarot specifically relates to the Tree of Life. Kabbalistic pathworking is an efficient method of guided meditation that facilitates balanced psychic development.

Suggested Reading: Regardie and Ciceros, *A Garden of Pomegranates, Skrying on the Tree of Life.*

Suggested Reading: Regardie and Ciceros, *The Middle Pillar, the Balance Between Mind & Magic.*

Suggested Reading: Stavish, *Kabbalah for Health and Wellness.*

Kirlian Photography. See Electrophotography. A method for photographing the etheric aura around plant and animal parts.

Suggested Reading: Krippner and Rubin, *The Kirlian Aura—Photographing the Galaxies of Life.*

Kundalini. The life force rising from the base of the spine, the *muladhara* chakra, and animating the body, our sexuality, the etheric body, and passing through the chakras to join with its opposite force descending through *sahasrara* chakra to open our higher consciousness. Psychic skills often accompany Kundalini arousal.

Suggested Reading: Mumford, *A Chakra & Kundalini Workbook: Psycho-spiritual Techniques for Health, Rejuvenation, Psychic Powers & Spiritual Rejuvenation.*

Suggested Reading: Paulson, *Kundalini and the Chakras: Evolution in this Lifetime—A Practical Guide.*

Levitation. Non-supported elevation of physical objects and persons. (1) Partial elevation is common to table-tipping in which the attendees place fingers lightly on a table and ask questions of supposed spirit presences. The table responds by lifting two or three of the four legs and tapping answers. (2) In some cases, the entire table has elevated.(3) During spiritual séances, various objects are sometimes elevated and move about the séance room. (4) During séances, the medium has actually been elevated and even moved outside the room through one window and returned through another. (5) During meditation and prayer, some people bounce and in other cases fully levitate.

L-Field, or Life Field. A weak electric field surrounding every living organism which acts like a matrix to guide its development. It is the etheric body, home to some psychic phenomena.

Life Between Lives. Following the belief in reincarnation, there is a period between the previous life and the next life during which the past life is reviewed and the next life planned.

Suggested Reading: Newton, *Destiny of Souls: New Case Studies of Life Between Lives.*

Suggested Reading: Newton, *Journey of Souls: Case Studies of Life Between Lives.*

Suggested Reading: Newton, *Life Between Lives: Hypnotherapy for Spiritual Regression.*

Life Purpose: We are here to grow, to become more than we are. Each of us has the ability to apply our inherent powers and our emerging skills to the challenge of accelerating personal growth. Much of this relates to psychic skills.

Light. In John 1:1–4 of the Christian Bible, it says:

In the beginning was the Word, and the Word was
With God, and the Word was God.
The same was in the beginning with God.
All things were made by him; and without him was not
Any thing made that was made.
In him was life; and the life was the light of men.

Here the "light" of men is identified with life. We know what light is—we see natural light every day and artificial light whenever we flip the switch. And we know that sunlight is essential to life, but this statement seems to be saying something additional: that life is, or was, the light of men. Light has an alternative meaning, as when we turn light on the subject, which identifies that aspect of directed consciousness that leads to intelligence about a subject. We see consciousness everywhere, but is it this particular aspect of focused, analytical, consciousness seemingly unique to humans that is the light of men?

Life evolves into new forms, but the statement seems to characterize the life of men as different than other life, and relates it to a particular kind of light. We speculate that this light of men is that of Soul Consciousness and is the light referred to in the word enlightenment.

Love. *In giving and receiving, there is love.* Love is one of the great mysteries. We *feel* love. Love is both something we project towards another, and then something that holds things together. It is an attractor force and a binding force. As humans, we yearn to give love and to receive love, and we speak of making love. As observers, we see the same phenomena out there in the world—not only in living things but in nonorganic things right down to the smallest particles. We think of love as an emotion, but it is unlike other emotions like fear and anger. We speak of "God's love," but we don't speak of "God's fear." Love is such a unique and powerful force that it almost takes on a physical dimension right along with the force of gravity, and perhaps it is love that is the unifying force that Einstein was searching for.

It is love that holds all the many parts together in a functional unity. Love brings people together in relationships, but it is also love that holds all the cells and organs and parts of the body together, and that holds all the many bodies (physical, psychic, emotional, mental, spiritual, and even extra-spiritual) together in the person each of us is. And it is love that allows us relationships with other dimensional beings and with our divine origin. There is no limit to love, as it is the creative force of the cosmos.

You can give this love other names if you prefer: attraction, gravity, magnetism, nuclear force, and others, but love is something we know. We experience the power of attraction, and we experience the yearning to love. We want to receive love and we want to give love. Through love, we seek expansion, to go beyond ourselves, to reach out towards union with the beloved, and through union we go beyond present limitations.

Lucid Dream. A particularly vivid dream in which the dreamer himself appears. It is believed to be a form of astral projection, and if the dreamer can take conscious control of dream it then becomes a full out-of-body experience.

Suggested Reading: McElroy *Lucid Dreaming for Beginners.*

Magic. The power to change things in conformity with will or desire. It is a function of focused consciousness accompanied by a force of love intending change reaching down into the universal field where everything exists as potential until affected by the operation of magic. This means that magic is happening all the time, but as magicians we have the opportunity and responsibility as co-creators to direct change in accordance with what is called the "Great Plan," meaning no more and no less than whatever the underlying purpose of creation is.

Magic Mirror. A device, similar to the crystal ball, to focus attention in a process of self-hypnosis to open a channel to the astral world, i.e., the subconscious mind.

Mana. The vital force that permeates everything. It is identical with ether and the astral light that fills space.

Manipura. The solar plexus chakra.

Mantra. A Sanskrit word or phrase rhythmically and repetitively chanted repetitively in meditation and prayer to induce a change in consciousness.

Martial Arts. A particular training of the whole person, and not just the physical body, uniting physical and psychic actions. See also Tao.

Suggested Reading: Carnie, *Chi Gung, Chinese Healing, Energy and Natural Magick.*

Materialization. When something appears as from nowhere. Apports reappear after being de-materialized and then re-materialized. It is also associated with poltergeist-like activity when stones appear in mid-air to fall on a house. Materializations of human forms or just of limbs and hands sometimes occur in séances, and wax impressions have been made of them.

Matrix. The background framework for all and any manifestation. It is a union of consciousness in the universal field of primary energy/matter potentials. The universal matrix is the pattern for the evolving universe and all within it. The individual matrix is the pattern of energy/matter guiding the development and function of each life form. It is mostly a function of mental, astral and etheric levels of consciousness guided by an intention expressed at the soul level. It functions as the etheric body.

Suggested Reading: Bradden, *The Divine Matrix—Bridging Time, Space, Miracles, and Belief.*

Meditation. (1) An emptying of the mind of all thoughts and chatter often by concentration only on the slow inhalation and exhalation of breath. It induces relaxation and a clean slate preparatory for receiving psychic impressions. (2) A careful thinking about a particular subject in a manner that brings access to physical memories as well as astral and mental level associations of knowledge about that subject. (3) A state of consciousness characterized by relaxed alertness reducing sensory impressions with increased receptivity to inner plane communications. Meditation is characterized by slow alpha and theta waves.

Suggested Reading: Clement, *Meditation for Beginners: Techniques for Awareness, Mindfulness & Relaxation.*

Suggested Reading: Paulson, *Meditation as Spiritual Practice.*

Medium. See also Channel. Most mediums enter a trance state and then—often through the agency of a control or guide—enable communication with a discarnate person. Often a control speaks for the spirit seeking communication.

Suggested Reading: Mathews, *Never Say Goodbye: A Medium's Stories of Connecting with Your Loved Ones.*

Mediumship. The study and development of the skill necessary to function as a spiritual medium facilitating communication between the worlds of spirit and the living. See also Spiritualism. Some mediums demonstrate various psychic skills, and séances are often accompanied by psychic phenomena.

Suggested Reading: Eynden, *So You Want to be a Medium? A Down-to-Earth Guide*. Woodbury, MN: Llewellyn Publications, 2006.

Mental Body. The fourth body. The lower mental body unites with the astral and etheric as the personality. The higher mental body is home to the Soul between incarnations.

Mental Plane. The third plane up from the physical/etheric. It is the plane where all thought is shared. It is the upper home for the Akashic records shared with the astral.

Mental Telepathy. Also called mind reading. The ability to read another person's thoughts, and even to carry on a mental conversation. See also Telepathy.

Meridians. Etheric level channels of energy within the body.

Monad. The fifth, or spiritual, body, which is separate from the personality and is a function of the Soul.

Mortal Soul. The astral body temporarily housing the soul after death of the physical body.

Muladhara. The base chakra.

Near-Death Experience (NDE). People near death, and sometimes those who have been resuscitated after dying, report common experiences of peacefulness followed by separation from the body. At first there is darkness, then a source of light and an awareness of moving into the light, sometimes through a tunnel. At this point, many turn back, or are turned to move back into the body. Sometimes they see family and friends, and other times a presence, who all advise that it is not yet the time for the person to pass over. Other times there may be a review of the lifetime and a decision made by the person to return to complete unfinished business. It is nearly always a very positive and transformative experience, giving the person a much greater appreciation of life.

Noosphere. The network of human thought surrounding the earth. See also Collective Unconscious.

Novus Ordo Seclorum. The New Order of the Ages represented in the Great Seal of the United States. N.O.S. is the spiritual unity behind the nation and the container for all the ideas represented by its founding. It has the potential to function as the over-soul of the nation should people turn inward to its inspiration. As we turn to the N.O.S. for inner guidance, it aligns us with those high ideas and guides their translation into their practical and contemporary manifestation. It is the repository of the high aspirations of the founding fathers and those thinkers and leaders who have sought to create a *new* nation based on principles rather than geographic and tribal boundaries. It represents the Spirit of America.

Occult. That which is, at least temporarily, hidden from our perception. In astronomy it refers to the passing of one body in front of another, as when the Moon passes in front of the Sun (an eclipse). In the common culture it has been used as a category for *hidden* knowledge, i.e., those subjects and technologies functioning to manifest psychic and spiritual faculties.

Suggested Reading: Greer, *The New Encyclopedia of the Occult.*

Occult Anatomy. The etheric matrix holding the physical body together, and the etheric and astral channels and organs that function to transfer and transform energies for the physical body and personality.

Od or Odic Force. It is an energy sometimes seen clairvoyantly surrounding living as well as material objects. It is comparable to the etheric body and etheric energy.

Operating System. Inside every computer there is a software package providing the instructions for the hardware to carry out the work requested by application software packages, such as Microsoft Word and Excel. The operating system is the interface between the computer hardware and the world, while the application packages are like the skills and training we learn by study and experience. Like every other computer, the human brain requires an operating system that interfaces with the world—our brain filters our perceptions to correspond to what we are conditioned to expect through parental guidance, our life experiences, education, training, and interaction with authority figures, social expectations, and, to a far lesser extent, by our genetic heritage and past-life memories. This operating system also conditions and directs the way we respond to external stimuli. Much of this operating system functions in the subconscious mind. Like computers, the operating system can be modified, updated, changed, and even replaced. Self-understanding is learning about our operating system; self-improvement is about modifying and changing our operating system; self-transformation is about updating and largely replacing our operating system.

Orgone. Another name for odic force, prana, ether, mana.

Ouija™ Board. A simple board with the alphabet printed on it, along with "yes" and "no," and a planchette or easily moveable device used to communicate with spirits. The users, usually two people of opposite gender, rest fingers on the planchette, which slides quickly to the various letters to spell out answers to questions.

Out-of-Body Experience (OBE). See Astral Projection.

Oversoul. The soul of the world.

Parakinesis. The movement of a far-too-heavy object by a person in a high emotional state who otherwise could not accomplish such a feat. The example is that of a mother lifting a heavy automobile to save her child from being crushed.

Paranormal. Parallel to the normal. Phenomena that is beyond the understanding of material science. While the paranormal is mostly confined to psychic-type events and experience, it also includes certain physical phenomena for which we do not as yet have an explanation.

Paraphernalia. Gadgets, tools, and equipment used in divinatory and magical operation, and the performance of religious ritual.

Parapsychologist. A person trained to study the paranormal and to explain paranormal phenomena from a psychological foundation.

Parapsychology. The scientific study of paranormal phenomena.

Past-Life Regression. A technique involving hypnosis, self-hypnosis or meditation to re-experience past-life events in order to resolve traumatic reactions, recover lost memories and skills, and resolve certain recurring problems.

Suggested Reading: Andrews, *How to Uncover Your Past Lives.*

Suggested Reading: Webster, *Practical Guide to Past Life Memories: Twelve Proven Methods.*

Pendulum. Simply a weight suspended on a string that is somewhat shorter than the length of the forearm. The string is held so that the weight can freely swing over a simple chart or map, or sometimes an object, and reveal by the direction of the swing answers to specific questions framed mostly for yes/no response. Bypassing conscious control, the subconscious provides the answers. Some people believe that spirits may move the pendulum similar to the movement of the planchette on the Ouija Board. Pendulums are also used in dowsing, often over a map with a sample of ore held in one hand or in a hollow cavity in the pendulum that serves as a witness to find a body of the same ore in the geographic location indicated by the pendulum over the map.

Suggested Reading: Ghiuselev, and Astanassov. *Pendulum Power Magic Kit.* Brass Pendulum, book, and full-color layout sheet to develop extrasensory faculties.

Perispirit. An alternate word for the Astral Body.

Personality. The immediate vehicle of personal consciousness we believe to be ourselves. It is a temporary complex drawn from the etheric, astral, and mental bodies containing current life memories, the current operating system,

Phantasm. An apparition of a living person, probably an astral projection.

Phantom. An apparition of a dead person, possibly the etheric/astral bodies after leaving the physical body.

Poltergeist. Literally, *a mischievous spirit.* A presence or energy, sometimes confined to a single room but more often associated with a particular person, that creates unintentional disturbances such as knocking over vases, clocks, mirrors, knicknacks, and other small but generally favorite objects. At one time, it was believed that the activity was the result of unstable emotional energies, often repressed, and unconsciously projected by adolescents during puberty.

Suggested Reading: Righi, *Ghosts, Apparitions and Poltergeists: An Exploration of the Supernatural through History.*

Possession. The temporary displacement of the self by a spirit entity. Possession can be voluntary, as when a medium surrenders her/his body to a spirit or involuntary when the entity takes over. In Voudoun, the god takes possession and rides the person like a horse. While the person is possessed, the body is often capable of physical feats beyond the normal ability of the person.

Post-Hypnotic Suggestion. A suggestion given during hypnotic trance for action to be taken after the subject returns to normal consciousness, often intended to change one habit (a negative one) to another habit (a positive one).

Power, the. Chi, Prana, life force, Kundalini. It refers in particular to the direction of personal energy combined with emotional force and conscious direct to bring about magical change.

Powers. The innate particular complexes of the etheric, astral, and mental bodies that manifest in conscious perceptions and actions sometimes called occult, paranormal, supernatural, or spiritual.

Prana. Chi, the Force, the Power. The universal life energy flowing throughout the universe. It can be visualized as flowing into the body as you inhale, and then distributed throughout the body as you exhale.

Prayer. (1) A mantra-like series of words addressed to deity to seek a particular benevolence and blessing. (2) An emotionally laden plea to deity to meet a personal or collective need. (3) A form of affirmation used in meditation, ritual ,or self-hypnosis to invoke the power of the subconscious mind to bring about change in personal circumstances.

Suggested Reading: Bradden, *Secrets of the Lost Mode of Prayer.*

Precognition. The psychic awareness of the future, to include knowledge of events, trends, and conditions.

Premonition. Like a hunch, it is usually an advance warning, a presentiment of something undesirable that will occur in the future.

Presence. A feeling that an invisible someone or something is present. It is generally felt to be a psychic sensitivity to a ghost or energy.

Preservation of Peak Growth. A phenomenon in which one's past peak of development is regained at death.

Suggested Reading: *Slate, Beyond Reincarnation: Experience Your Past Lives & Lives Between Lives.*

PSI. Psychic phenomena.

Psychic Attack. An attack on the astral body which will cause an effect on the physical body as well. It may be intentional but other times it is caused by strong emotions of hatred, greed, envy, lust, etc., directed toward the victim. See Psychic Self-Defense.

Psychic Body. Generally conceived as the etheric and astral bodies together.

Psychic Guide. See Spirit Guide.

Psychic Powers. All the abilities, especially as trained skills, associated with the paranormal, including astral projection, aura reading, channeling, clairaudience, clairvoyance, extrasensory perception, mediumship, mental telepathy, psychokinesis, remote viewing, spirit communication, spiritual healing, telekinesis, teleportation, etc.

Suggested Reading: Denning and Phillips, *Practical Guide to Psychic Powers: Awaken Your Sixth Sense.*

Suggested Reading: Webster, *Psychic Development for Beginners: An Easy Guide to Releasing and Developing Your Psychic Abilities.*

Psychic Self-Defense. Techniques and practices to build psychic defenses against psychic predators, skilled advertisers and salespeople, emotional manipulators, and psychic attack.

Suggested Reading: Denning and Phillips, *Practical Guide to Psychic Self-Defense: Strengthen Your Aura.*

Suggested Reading: Penczak, *A Witch's Shield: Protection Magick and Psychic Self-Defense.*

Psychic Vampires. Some people, usually unknowingly, extract energy—not blood—from living people around them. In most cases, such as politicians and entertainers working with crowds, this goes unnoticed, but between individuals this can be devastating.

Suggested Reading: Slate, *Psychic Vampires: Protection from Energy Predators and Parasites.*

Psychokinesis (PK). The movement of objects without physical contact.

Psychometry. The reading of emotional and psychic energies impressed on an object such as a watch, jewelry, etc., to reveal its history and ownership.

Suggested Reading: Andrews, *How to Do Psychic Readings through Touch.*

Psychoplasm. Alternative for Ectoplasm.

Psychotronics. Alternative for Parapsychology.

Radionics. The study of the radiations sensed by dowsers, and further developed to measure radiations from the physical/etheric body.

Raps and Rapping. Noises produced during a séance, seeming to come from the surface of tables, walls, ceilings, floors. The sounds seem to be some kind of energy materialization produced by a spirit to announce its presence and sometimes as a means of communication.

Reality. The personal world as seen through our belief system. While it mostly coincides with that of other people, self-analysis will show deviations and distortions reflecting the feelings of the person.

Regression. The recovery of past memories through hypnosis or meditation.

Reincarnation. The belief that the Soul experiences multiple lives through newly born physical bodies and personalities. Upon death of the physical body, the personality withdraws to the astral and then mental plane while the essential lessons of that incarnation are abstracted to the soul.

Suggested Reading: Slate, *Beyond Reincarnation: Experience your Past Lives & Lives Between Lives.*

Rejuvenation. The condition of becoming youthful again, or the process of making a person young or youthful again.

Suggested Reading: Slate, *Rejuvenation: Strategies for Living Younger, Longer & Better.*

Remote Viewing. Viewing at a distance by psychic means. The debate continues whether this is a form of Astral Projection, or simple Clairvoyance.

Retrocognition. Psychic knowledge of the past.

Sahasrara. The crown chakra.

Scrying. Sometimes spelled Skrying. The psychic techniques of reaching into the subconscious mind by means of focusing devices, such as crystal balls, magic mirrors, pendulums, dowsing rods, shells, oracular dreaming, Ouija™ boards, aura reading, psychometry, automatic writing, and speaking.

Suggested Reading: Tyson, *Scrying for Beginners: Tapping into the Supersensory Powers of Your Subconscious.*

Seance. A group, usually as a circle, gathered together to give energy support to a person functioning as a medium serving as an intermediary in communication between the world of spirits of the deceased and living people.

Self-Hypnosis. The self-induction of hypnotic trance and the practice of self-programming through simple affirmations mostly expressed as already accomplished "I AM" conditions, such as "I AM slim."

Suggested Reading: Park, *Get Out of Your Way, Unlocking the Power of Your Mind to Get What You Want,* with audio CD for self-hypnosis.

Shamanic Practices. The projection of conscious awareness into the astral world accomplished through trance induction by methods of physical stress including fasting, sleep deprivation, ecstatic dancing, flagellation, prolonged bondage, sensory deprivation, sensory overload, drumming, and the use of hallucinogenic and psychoactive substances.

Suggested Reading: Walsh, *The World of Shamanism: New Views of an Ancient Tradition.*

Sigil. A personal ideogram condensing a written affirmation used to magically accomplish a particular objective.

Skills. Trained powers.

Soul. The essential self behind all personal manifestation. It is not the personality but it absorbs the core lessons learned in the life of each personality created in a series of incarnations.

Spirit. Used variously to identify (1) the Spiritual Body, or Soul; (2) the essence of the deceased person in communication with the living or appearing as a ghost; (3) entities from other dimensions or planets channeling to humans; (4) nonhuman inhabitants of the astral plane; (5) a collective term for nonindividual spiritual power and intelligence, probably an aspect of the collective unconscious or universal consciousness. In addition, there is the Holy Spirit, which may be the primal consciousness or matrix that can be activated by prayer or other affirmative thoughts.

Spirit Communication. Generally, the communication between living people and the spirits of the deceased. Also may include communication with other spiritual entities—guides, angels, masters, etc.

Suggested Reading: Buckland, *Buckland's Book of Spirit Communications.*

Suggested Reading: Konstantinos, *Speak with the Dead: Seven Methods for Spirit Communication.*

Spirit Guide. An entity manifesting on the astral or mental plane exhibiting high intelligence and wisdom with a personal interest in the welfare of the individual experiencing the more or less constant presence of the guide.

Suggested Reading: Andrews, *How to Meet and Work with Spirit Guides.*

Suggested Reading: Webster, *Spirit Guides & Angel Guardians: Contact Your Invisible Helpers.*

Spiritism. A distinction made from spiritualism to include the African-derived religions involving communication and possession by gods rather than spirits of the deceased.

Spiritual Body. The fifth body, also called the Monad.

Spiritual Genotype. The individual's unique spiritual or cosmic makeup which remains unchanged from lifetime to lifetime.

Suggested Reading: Slate, *Beyond Reincarnation: Experience your Past Lives & Lives Between Lives.*

Spiritualism. Generally the practice and the religion associated with spirit mediumship and communication and belief in the survival of the individual after physical death as spirit.

Sub-Atomic Field. Also called simply the Field, in which primal/universal energy and matter appear as waves and then as particles when observed. It is the foundation for the study of quantum physics (also called quantum mechanics and quantum theory). Packets of energy/matter are called quanta.

Subconsciousness. Also called "the Unconscious." It is the *lower* part of the personality containing forgotten and repressed feelings and memories, Feelings and the fundamental Belief or Operating System that filters reality, that collection of guilt feelings called the Shadow, the anima or animus collection of feelings representing our idealization or fear and hatred of the opposite gender, the various archetypes and mythic images formed though the history of human experience, all of which can operate as doorways or gates to the astral world and connect to the higher or super consciousness. The subconscious is also home to our instincts and the autonomic system that cares for the body and its operation. The subconscious mind is accessed by various techniques including hypnosis, prayer, and ritual, and during sleep.

Success Expectations. Success means goals accomplished. Success is not only measured financially but by having met or exceeded your expectations and hopes in your endeavors. It can be found in your career, in your study program, in your hobbies, in your relationships, and in your personal growth and development program. It is a strong and inclusive word. "I AM successful" is a dynamic and powerful affirmation. "You're a success" is a beautiful commendation. Success expectations are what we create in connection with our goals, the carrot that pulls us forward. Always establish what your success expectations are and keep them in the forefront of your consciousness.

Super Conscious Mind. The *higher* level of personal consciousness with access to the universal of collective unconscious. It is where the gods or powerful archetypes and spirit guides can be found, and where the Akashic records are accessed.

Supernatural. Literally, beyond the natural, used to describe psychic and spiritual experience. Since we don't believe anything can be not natural, we extend our science to gain understanding of such phenomena.

Svadhisthana. The sacral chakra.

Table-Tilting, Table-Lifting, Table-Turning. The partial or complete lifting of a table in a séance setting used in communication (most in response to yes/no questions with one tilt or two) with spirits.

Tao. Taoism is a Chinese philosophical system in which the Tao is both the ultimate reality in which all action takes place, the way by which an individual can live in harmony with the universe, and the universal energy behind all phenomena.

Tarot. A vast system of archetypal knowledge condensed into a system of seventy-eight images on cards that can be finger-manipulated and then laid out in systematic patterns to answer specific questions or provide guidance to the solution of problems. While it is a form of divination, it is one of the most sophisticated and carefully developed systems of images and relationships following the structure of the Kabbalah's Tree of Life. Going beyond divination, it is also a system to access the unconscious, and to structure magical ritual. It's a powerful Western esoteric system comparable to the Eastern I Ching.

Suggested Reading: Amber K, and Azrael Arynn K., *Heart of Tarot: an Intuitive Approach.*

Suggested Reading: Ferguson, *The Llewellyn Tarot*, deck and book.

Suggested Reading: Moore, *What Tarot Can Do for You: Your Future In the Cards.*

Suggested Reading: Tyson, *1-2-3 Tarot: Answers In an Instant.*

Telekinesis. The psychic skill to move the location or change the shape of a physical object. See Psychokinesis.

Telepathy. See Mental Telepathy. Mind-to-mind communication or thought reading, more commonly experienced during trance.

Teleportation. The de-materialization of a person and re-materialization at a different location.

Thaumaturgy. Also called low and practical magic. It is the magic of external things.

Theurgy. Also called high magic (or magick) that deals with raising the level of consciousness and the fulfillment of the great plan of man's evolution and reunion with the ultimate Source.

Thought. Astral and mental collections expressed mostly in words to represent a particular opinion, intention, or plan of action. We *think* thoughts. We *feel* emotions.

Thought Form. (1) A concentrated mental image created by a magician to accomplish a specified objective. (2) A spontaneous image created in the imagination that is charged with emotional energy. Either is perceived by a clairvoyant and is felt by ordinary people with some degree of psychic sensitivity. A carefully constructed mental image that is charged with emotional energy can become a manipulative tool used in product marketing, political action, and religious domination.

Suggested Reading: Ashcroft-Nowicki and Brennan, *Magical Use of Thought Forms: A Proven System of Mental & Spiritual Empowerment.*

Trance. A state of consciousness in which awareness has turned inward to the subconscious mind either unconsciously through repetitive stimuli or consciously induced in a similar technique in hypnosis, meditation, or religious or shamanic practice. During a trance state, carefully prepared programs of suggestion and affirmation can lead to dramatic changes in conscious behavior and perceptions.

UFOs. Unidentified Flying Objects or flying saucers. After seventy or more years of observations, there is no certainty about the nature of these paranormal phenomena. While the appearance is physical and suggestive of superior technology of alien origin, the UFO experience has taken on a mythic quality. Some people speculate that UFOs have the same role as angels in seeming to represent some higher power interested in humanity and perhaps the salvation of the earth's well-being; others see a similarity between the UFO and such paranormal phenomena as the Loch Ness Monster, medieval dragons, Abominable Snowmen, and Sasquatch. The sudden appearance and sudden disappearance of all these things suggests a particular kind of psychic sensitivity in which entities from the lower astral world temporarily appear to the physical perception.

Suggested Reading: Danelek, *UFOs: The Great Debate, An Objective Look at Extraterrestrials, Government Cover-ups, and the Prospect for First Contact.*

Suggested Reading: Greer, *The UFO Phenomenon: Fact, Fantasy and Disinformation.*

Unconscious. (1) A lack of consciousness. (2) An alternate word for the subconscious mind. (3) A particular reference to the *personal* Unconscious region of the mind where suppressed desires, memories, and feelings reside. In common usage, the personal unconscious is somewhat lesser than the subconscious mind. Some theoreticians believe that at least some psychic phenomena rise from these areas of the personality as *quanta* of energy/matter packets manifesting in poltergeist-like phenomena.

Universal Force. The force, the Tao, the energy behind all existence, physical and otherwise.

Vishuddha. The throat chakra.

Visualization. Using the imagination to create vivid images of desired conditions or objects to attract those goals. Visualizations are sometimes perceived by the clairvoyant and may be used to contain psychic powers. Creative visualization is a practical system for personal success.

Yantra. A particular geometric-style of diagram from Tantric philosophy believed to represent and contain specific psychic energies. Meditation on the Yantra will induce specific consciousness experiences.

Yoga. An Indian system, like Taoism and Western Magick, intended to develop the whole person, including the psychic and spiritual bodies.

Suggested Reading: Mumford, and Riddle, *Yoga Nidra, Chakra Theory & Visualization.*

Suggested Reading: Muni, *Yoga: the Ultimate Spiritual Path.*

Zero Point Field. See Field.

INDEX

Skill, 2, 44, 75–76, 168, 195, 201, 213

Slate, Joe H., 7, 22

Sleep, 15–16, 47, 59–62, 93, 97–99, 101–103, 105–106, 113, 127–129, 148, 150, 154, 180, 184, 186, 191, 209, 211

Sleep Arrest Program, 93

Sleep-induced astral travel, 101

Sleep on it, 15–16

Slowing aging, 76, 175, 194

Software, 57, 62, 203

Solar plexus, 72, 176, 188, 200

Soul, 8, 57, 85, 87, 115, 119, 123, 137–138, 144–146, 150, 168, 176, 185–186, 196, 199, 201–204, 208, 210

Source, 4, 6, 56, 71–72, 103, 106, 115, 119, 123, 128, 133, 136, 142, 144, 146, 152, 154, 164–166, 168, 170–171, 174, 188, 193–194, 202, 213

Spirit, 5, 19, 55, 57–59, 63, 71, 82, 86, 94, 103, 115–116, 118–121, 123–132, 137, 145, 152, 155, 158, 164, 173, 179, 190–192, 195, 197, 201, 203, 205–208, 210–212

Spirit communication, 19, 120, 207, 210

Spirit guide, 103, 126, 129, 131, 207, 210

Spiritism, 211

Spiritual, 2–3, 6, 8, 22–23, 43, 46, 51, 53, 57, 65, 67, 69, 98, 115–116, 118–123, 125–128, 130–131, 137, 142, 145–146, 152–153, 155, 161, 169, 171, 173, 175–176, 178, 186–188, 197–199, 201–203, 206–207, 210–213, 215

Spiritual attainment, 22

Spiritual body, 3, 145, 202, 210–211

Spiritual genotype, 211

Spiritual growth, 43, 173

Spiritual plane, 155

Spiritualism, 189, 201, 211

Spiritual technologies, 65

State of being, 58, 65

States of consciousness, 22, 28, 32, 58, 62, 147–148, 184–185

Statistical analysis, 34

Sub-atomic, 211

Subconscious mind, 61, 139, 141–142, 149–150, 165, 171–172

Subconscious powers, 40, 78, 103

Subconscious resources, 82, 85, 102, 104, 195

Subtle body, 144, 185

Subtle fluid, 154

Success, 6–10, 12, 18, 24, 33, 35–36, 43–45, 47–48, 52–54, 76–77, 79–80, 89, 93–94, 100, 102–103, 109, 111, 113, 172–173, 175, 178, 180–181, 187, 193, 211–212, 215

Success expectations, 211–212

LLEWELLYN ORDERING INFORMATION

Order Online:
Visit our website at www.llewellyn.com, select your books, and order them on our secure server.

Order by Phone:
- Call toll-free within the U.S. at 1-877-NEW-WRLD (1-877-639-9753). Call toll-free within Canada at 1-866-NEW-WRLD (1-866-639-9753)
- We accept VISA, MasterCard, and American Express

Order by Mail:
Send the full price of your order (MN residents add 6.875% sales tax) in U.S. funds, plus postage & handling to:

> **Llewellyn Worldwide**
> **2143 Wooddale Drive, Dept. 978-0-7387-1893-4**
> **Woodbury, MN 55125-2989**

Postage & Handling:

Standard (U.S., Mexico, & Canada). If your order is:
$24.99 and under, add $4.00
$25.00 and over, FREE STANDARD SHIPPING

AK, HI, PR: $16.00 for one book plus $2.00 for each additional book.

International Orders (airmail only):
$16.00 for one book plus $3.00 for each additional book

Orders are processed within 2 business days.
Please allow for normal shipping time. Postage and handling rates subject to change.

Aura Energy for Health, Healing & Balance
Joe H. Slate, Ph.D.

Imagine an advanced energy/information system that contains the chronicle of your life—past, present, and future. By referring to it, you could discover exciting new dimensions to your existence. You could uncover important resources for new insights, growth, and power.

You possess such a system right now. It is your personal aura. In his latest book, Dr. Joe H. Slate illustrates how each one of us has the power to see the aura, interpret it, and fine-tune it to promote mental, physical, and spiritual well-being. College students have used his techniques to raise their grade-point averages, gain admission to graduate programs, and eventually get the jobs they want. Now you can use his aura empowerment program to initiate an exciting new spiral of growth in all areas of your life.

978-1-56718-637-6, 264 pp., 6 x 9 $14.95

Astral Travel for Beginners

Transcend Time and Space with Out-of-Body Experiences

RICHARD WEBSTER

Astral projection, or the out-of-body travel, is a completely natural experience. You have already astral traveled thousands of times in your sleep, you just don't remember it when you wake up. Now, you can learn how to leave your body at will, be fully conscious of the experience, and remember it when you return.

The exercises in this book are carefully graded to take you step-by-step through an actual out-of-body experience. Once you have accomplished this, it becomes easier and easier to leave your body. That's why the emphasis in this book is on your first astral travel.

The ability to astral travel can change your life. You will have the freedom to go anywhere and do anything. You can explore new worlds, go back and forth through time, make new friends, and even find a lover on the astral planes. Most importantly, you will find that you no longer fear death as you discover that you are indeed a spiritual being independent of your physical body.

By the time you have finished the exercises in this book you will be able to leave your body and explore the astral realms with confidence and total safety.

978-1-56718-796-0, 256 pp., 5³⁄₁₆ x 8 $12.95

To order, call 1-877-NEW-WRLD
Prices subject to change without notice
Order at Llewellyn.com 24 hours a day, 7 days a week!

A Chakra & Kundalini Workbook

Psycho-Spiritual Techniques for Health, Rejuvenation,
Psychic Powers and Spiritual Realization

Dr. Jonn Mumford (Swami Anandakapila Saraswati)

Spend just a few minutes each day on the remarkable psycho-physiological techniques in this book and you will quickly build a solid experience of drugless inner relaxation that will lead toward better health, a longer life, and greater control over your personal destiny.

Furthermore, you will lay a firm foundation for the subsequent chapters leading to the attainment of supernormal powers (i.e., photographic memory, self-anesthesia, and mental calculations), an enriched inner life, and ultimate transcendence. Learn techniques to use for burnout, mild to moderate depression, insomnia, general anxiety, and panic attacks, and reduction of mild to moderate hypertension. Experience sex for consciousness expansion, ESP development, and positive thinking. The text is supplemented with tables and illustrations to bridge the distance from information to personal understanding. In addition, the author has added a simple outline of a twelve-week practice schedule referenced directly back to the first nine chapters.

A Chakra & Kundalini Workbook is one of the clearest, most approachable books on yoga there is. Tailored for the Western mind, this is a practical system of personal training suited for anyone in today's active and complex world.

978-1-56718-473-0, 288 pp., 6 x 9 $21.95

To order, call 1-877-NEW-WRLD
Prices subject to change without notice
Order at Llewellyn.com 24 hours a day, 7 days a week!

Dream Exploration

A New Approach

ROBERT P. GONGLOFF

Dreams speak to us in a symbolic language. From night to night, those symbols and images can appear wildly different. But in truth, they are likely replaying an important theme in your life, a vital message from your dream world to your conscious mind.

While most dream books focus on symbolism, *Dream Exploration* helps readers go deeper by exploring the themes presented in dream life and their relationship to waking life. Written as a how-to guide, this first-of-its-kind book includes a twelve-step process that helps you identify core themes in your life and how best to grow with them. Also included is a theme matrix that offers practical actions readers can take to move beyond their dreams.

978-0-7387-0818-8, 192 pp., 5³⁄₁₆ x 8 $12.95